GW01018619

FALCOT'S

WEAVE COMPENDIUM

420801

FALCOT'S

WEAVE
COMPENDIUM

A Source Book for
Textile Designers and Weavers

P. Falcot

Edited & Introduced by

Ann Sutton

Translated by

Anne Satow

A Deirdre McDonald Book
Bellew Publishing
London

Grateful acknowledgement is made to
PETER COLLINGWOOD and JAMES PARK
for their help in checking the text.

Published in 1990 by
Deirdre McDonald Books
Bellew Publishing Co. Ltd
7 Southampton Place, London WC1A 2DR

Introduction and caption copyright © by Ann Sutton 1990

All rights reserved

Designed by Bob Vickers and Eric Drewery

ISBN 0 947792 51 1

Printed and bound in England
by
Mackays of Chatham

CONTENTS

PART II – PEG-PLANS

vi

INTRODUCTION

Sometimes, when researching for a book, you discover an out-of-print volume in a library which is so relevant, so desirable, that your law-abiding upbringing goes out of the window and you are shocked to be hatching plans for smuggling it out past the all-seeing electronic eye. Demons in your head reason (a) that it is unlikely to be appreciated if left on these inhospitable library shelves and (b) that outside in the world, with you, it can once again make a contribution to life. Monsieur P. Falcot's *Treatise on Weaving* was such a temptation.

While researching for our book *Ideas in Weaving*, Diane Sheehan and I discovered the charms, wisdom and value of M. Falcot's splendid collection. Published in 1852, in Mulhouse, the two volumes (one of plates, the other of text) store generous knowledge of the finest hours of the handweaver in France, a country which was then world-renowned for its fine woven fabrics and the ingenuity of its textile processes. 'Ideas' tumble out of its pages. Neglected and forgotten techniques are explained in its clear diagrams. We soon realized that it contained endless possibilities for handweavers today, and that the loom-adapting, gadget-building weaver (or, more usually, weaver's spouse) would have a field day.

Once we knew about these volumes, life without them became intolerable. The next (honest) step was to organize a reprint, but this solution was impossible without access to the originals. We composed persuasive letters to librarians, but were too pessimistic even to send them. And then the Gods smiled: led by a New York weave-designer friend to a Paris bookshop which was reputedly textile-friendly, I spotted the magic volumes on a shelf, and beat the world speed record to pay for them. When my New York friend saw them, she said: 'I'll pay you to get that second part photocopied.' She confirmed our belief that M. Falcot's volume of plates contains *two* hoards of treasure: Part One, with its technical revelations and pointers towards the rethinking and ideas-generating which are necessary to fuel the important craft of weaving today; and Part Two, an unprecedented collection of over 1,500 weave patterns, culminating in bands of adjacent weaves, juxtaposed by experts. Although fascinating to all weavers, this collection is particularly valuable to the growing groups of 'complex weave' enthusiasts, *and now more than ever before*, because these peg-plans form the data for which every computerized weaver constantly searches. The programme which I use ('Design & Weave' by J. and H. Lazennec, via A.V.L.) enables me to 'overlap' two peg-plans and to see the serendipitous result; endless fun for happy weavers, but it needs to be fed with good meals of peg-plan data. It will never be hungry again. I like to think that M. Falcot is happy and amused at this new need for his painstaking collection. Although he devotes a reverential chapter to the work of M. Charles Marie Jacquard, neither of these brilliant men could have foreseen the development of M. Jacquard's pattern-weaving device into the breath-taking computerized application of today. It is significant that M. Falcot's collection of weave structures should be feeding the computers of weave designers over one hundred years after his death: I am sure he would be pleased.

The Selection of Plates Included in Section I of this Facsimile

Although the two sturdy volumes which comprise the original work would be fascinating in their entirety for most weavers, selection was obviously necessary if today's weavers were to be able to afford to own the reprint. Although the French text is sound and informative, it was felt that the details relevant to the plates could be extracted and translated and for this I am grateful for the help of Anne Satow who has great knowledge of both weaving *and* the French language.

In making a selection from the 225 plates contained in the first part of the original volume of plates, the main criterion was the general interest of each plate. The book was first published in the heyday of handweaving, just as power looms were rearing their threatening heads. Handweaving was at its most ingenious, so those plates which show equipment and tools were retained. Out went the scores of *'esquisses'* – sketch designs for textiles – which, although indeed exquisite, are not relevant to handweaving today. Endless threading drafts for taffetas, satins and serges were also discarded. Esoteric variations on Jacquard looms were omitted, as were most Jacquard point-paper designs. Regretfully, plates of early power looms had to be left out also. Apologies to those weavers whose studies seem to be terminated abruptly by a 'missing' plate: recourse to Falcot's original volumes may reveal the information required.

The second half of the book has been retained in its entirety – every one of the 1,579 weave structures is here. (It comes as almost a pleasant shock to realize that Monsieur P. Falcot was as human as any of us, and *made mistakes* in his drafts: better check that the weaves repeat accurately when using them today.)

How to Use the Second Half of this Book

The presentation of weaves in the form of 'peg-plans' may at first confuse any weaver who is uncertain about extracting information from them. (As always, more designs will be utilized by owners of multi-harness looms than by those whose looms have four shafts or less.) The computer-aided loom is generally based on the traditional 'dobby', where sequences of lifts are programmed in and present themselves automatically. Before computer-aid, each lift was programmed by inserting pegs (often of wood) into the relevant holes in wooden 'lags', which were joined together in a continuous 'chain', each lag representing one pick in the repeat. The person inserting the pegs was guided by a point-paper diagram known as the peg-plan, which always had the same number of squares across as the number of shafts needed for that design.

A weave needing eight shafts could look like this (with eight lags):

 Fig. 1

or like this (with sixteen lags):

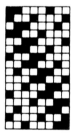 Fig. 2

In theory, there is no limit to the number of lags in a chain. In traditional practice, the tedious pegging process, the weight of the completed chain and, probably, the shortage of actual lags tend to ensure a reasonable length to the pattern repeat. M. Falcot is kind enough to label his plates so that we can select the ones suitable for our looms: '4 sur 4', '4 sur 12'. '4 sur 20' are of use to all of us with four-shaft table looms; '19 sur 19', '20 sur 30' will please those who have multi-shaft looms; '35 sur 35' and '40 sur 40' may serve only as inspiration, to be adapted for simpler equipment.

The majority of weavers who are not accustomed to working from peg-plans (and who weave on floor looms) should regard the plan as a weave diagram for the number of shafts on their loom. Apply a simple procedure to the plan which will give you the threading, tie-up and order of treadling.

Example based on '4 sur 8', No.44 (see p.110).
(a) Copy it on to point paper (see Fig.3a).
(b) Repeat it three times, to the right and below, to check the accuracy of the repeat (see Fig.3b).
(c) On the single repeat, work out the threading necessary for this design. Examining the columns a, b, c, d (see Fig.3c), it will be seen that each column bears a different combination of marks. Indicate this by an X above each column, on different rows. This design, therefore, needs a straight entry (see Fig.3d).
(d) Examine each horizontal row in turn (1 to 8 on Fig.3c). In row 1, shafts 2 and 3 need to be lifted; indicate this by 0's to the right of the threading X's. This is the tie-up. Each horizontal row is dealt with in turn, and where a combination of lifts is repeated this is indicated in the diagonal marks (representing the order of treadling) under the tie-up.

Fig. 3

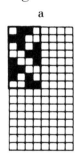
a

b

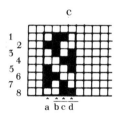
c
a b c d

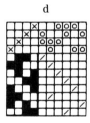
d

It will now be seen that this design can be woven on a four-shaft loom with six treadles.

It will be obvious that if the number of differing horizontal rows exceeds the number of treadles on your loom, you will be able to weave this pattern only on a table loom or dobby. (Owners of four-shaft floor looms may be able to use the single-tie method.) For those with eight-shaft floor looms, even with only eight treadles, there are still hundreds of patterns available to you in this book. And the growing swing towards computer-aided weaving will lead to greater and greater use of the whole of M. Falcot's unique collection.

X

TRAITÉ

ENCYCLOPÉDIQUE ET MÉTHODIQUE

DE LA

FABRICATION DES TISSUS,

PAR

P. FALCOT,

DESSINATEUR, PROFESSEUR DE THÉORIE-PRATIQUE POUR LA FABRICATION DE TOUS LES GENRES DE TISSUS,

MEMBRE DE LA SOCIÉTÉ D'ENCOURAGEMENT POUR L'INDUSTRIE NATIONALE.

DEUXIÈME ÉDITION,

Entièrement revue, corrigée, et augmentée de plus du double.

Ornée du portrait de Jacquard et de celui de l'auteur.

Accompagnée de 300 planches d'ustensiles, mécaniques, plans de machines, montages divers, dessins en esquisses et en mises en carte, etc., ainsi que d'un album contenant environ 2000 dessins brefs ou armures applicables à tous les genres de nouveautés.

Publication honorée de la souscription du Gouvernement.

OUVRAGE INDISPENSABLE

à toutes les personnes qui se vouent à la fabrication des tissus-nouveautés.

Prix : broché 50 francs.

TEXTE.

A ELBEUF (sur Seine), chez l'AUTEUR.
A MULHOUSE, chez J. P. RISLER, LIBRAIRE.

1852.

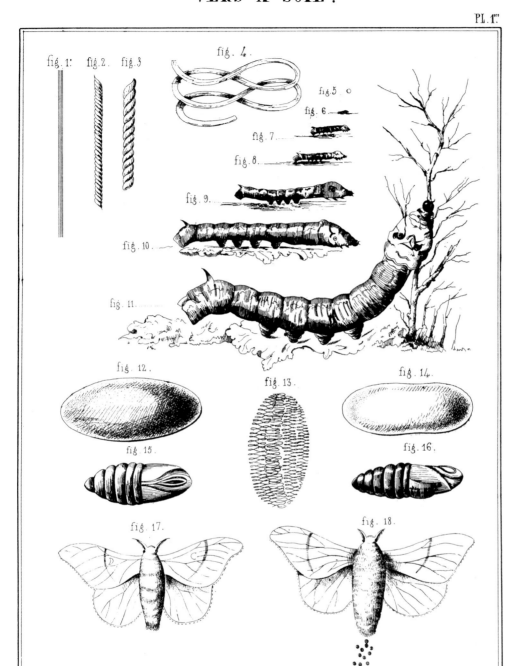

Traité des Tissus. 2ᵉ Édition.　　　　P. FALCOT.　　　　Lith. de B. Boehrer à Altkirch.

Plate 1 shows various stages in the life cycle of the silkworm, from the eggs (fig.5) through the development of the worm, with its voracious appetite, to the stage where it miraculously spins its silk cocoon (figs.12-16) with a continuous thread spun zigzag fashion round its body. Falcot sees the production of silk as being as mysterious as that of honey; 'indeed, perhaps silk is to the touch as honey is to taste; both seem more to flatter our senses than merely to satisfy our needs.'

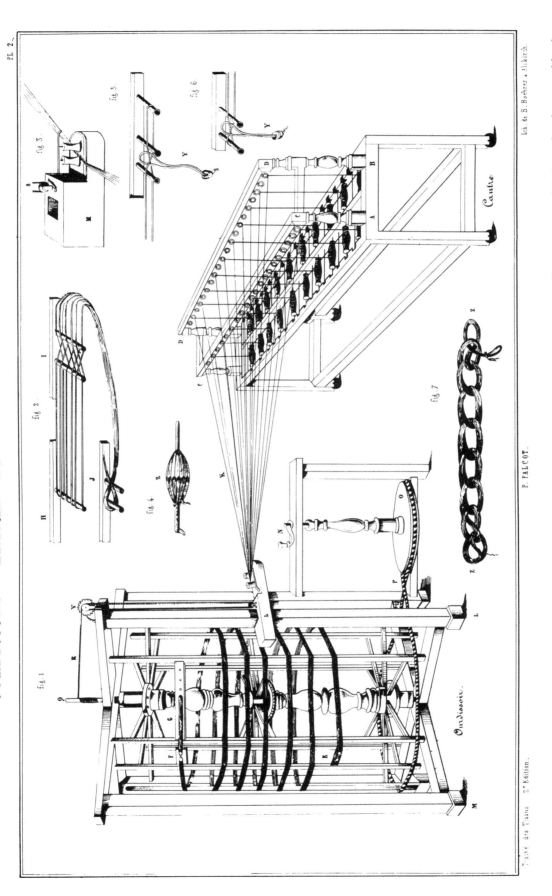

OURDISSOIR VERTICAL ET CANTRE LONGITUDINALE.

fig 1

fig 2

fig 3

fig 5

fig 6

fig 4

fig 7

Cantre.

Ourdissoir.

P. FALCOT.

Traité des Tissus. 2.ᵉ Édition.

Lith de B. Boehrer, Altkirch.

Plate 2 shows the most usual method of warping: a vertical warping mill with its accompanying horizontal creel. The warping mill is turned and reversed by the handle (N).

Two methods of removing the finished warp are shown – winding on to a stick, (fig.4) and chaining (fig.7). Warps for selvedges are made separately.

Plate 3 For beaming on, the warp is wound on to the large drum, starting with the single thread (front) cross. When wound, a stick and cord are put through to hold the heel end (portee cross end) straight, and the *musettes* (half-portees) are placed in the raddle dents – preferably one to a dent, but gaps can be left if

PLIAGE OU MONTOIR.

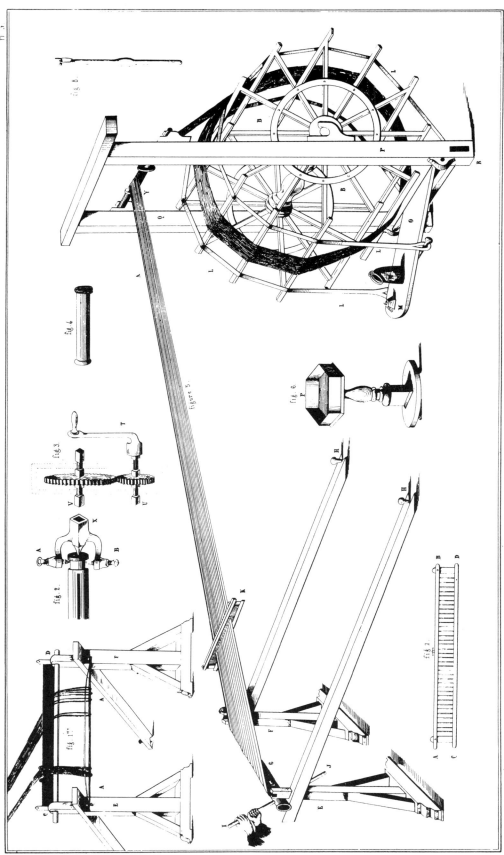

Traité des Tissus 2ᵉ Édition

P. FALCOT.

necessary to obtain the correct width. The slotted wooden bobbin (fig.4) is placed over the raddle as a support for the warp during this operation. The stick is placed on a frame (fig.5) close to the beam; one operator then turns the beam, and another holds the raddle and checks the warp as it passes through. A mechanical turning system is shown in figs. 2 and 3. Tension in the warp is maintained by the two straps L–L and variable weights.

Fig.8 shows the stick on which the warp had been wound from the warping mill. Alternatively, if it had been taken off as a chain, the revolving table (fig.6) would have supported it while it was being wound on to the wheel.

6

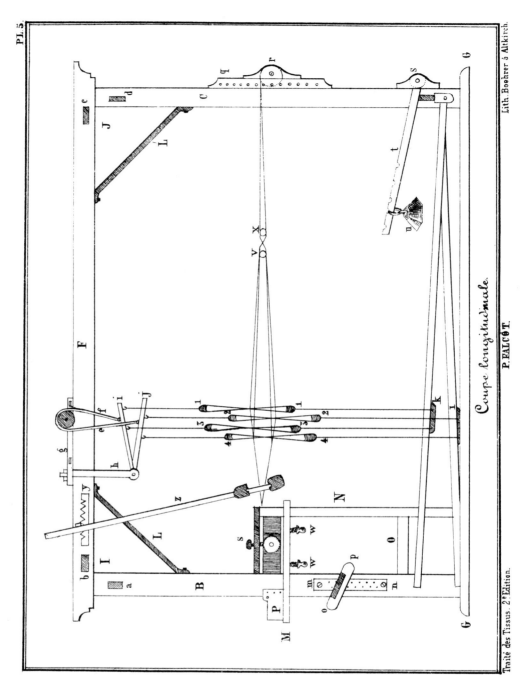

MÉTIER À TISSER

PI.5

Coupe longitudinale.

P. FALCOT.

Lith. Boehrer à Altkirch.

Traité des Tissus. 2ᵉ Édition.

Plates 5 and 6 show the elevations of a standard loom frame from the side (Plate 5) and front and back (Plate 6). The basic structure for a loom varies little apart from the width and length; it is the accessories, depending on the cloth to be woven, which vary. The diagrams are mainly self-explanatory. In Plates 5 and 6, P is a small box, one at each side, for keeping spare bobbins and pirns. Iron braces L helped keep the loom in shape, but for heavier fabrics heavier bracing would be needed.

These are silk looms, having no breast-beam. (As the cloth builds up on the front beam so the back beam is adjusted upwards; see Plate 10.) S (on Plate 6) is the adjustable seat, fastened to the loom by means of the detailed attachment shown in Plate 10.

MÉTIER À TISSER.

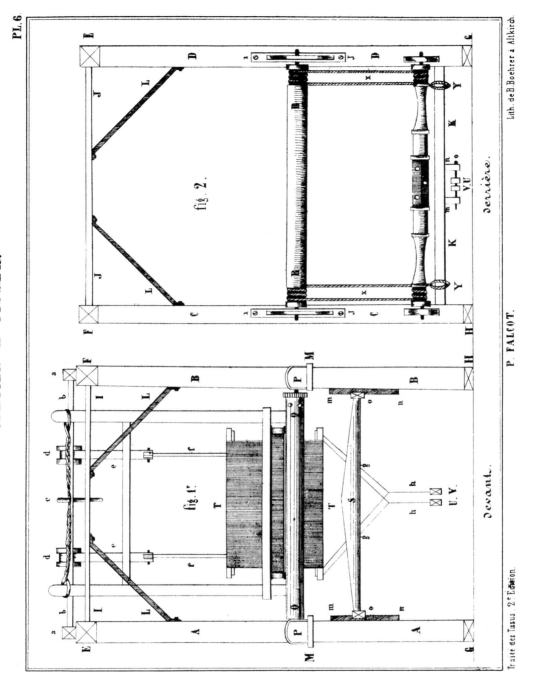

fig. 2.

derrière.

fig. 1.ᵉ

Devant.

Lith. de B. Boehrer à Altkirch.

Traité des Tissus. 2ᵉ Édition.

P. FALCOT.

8

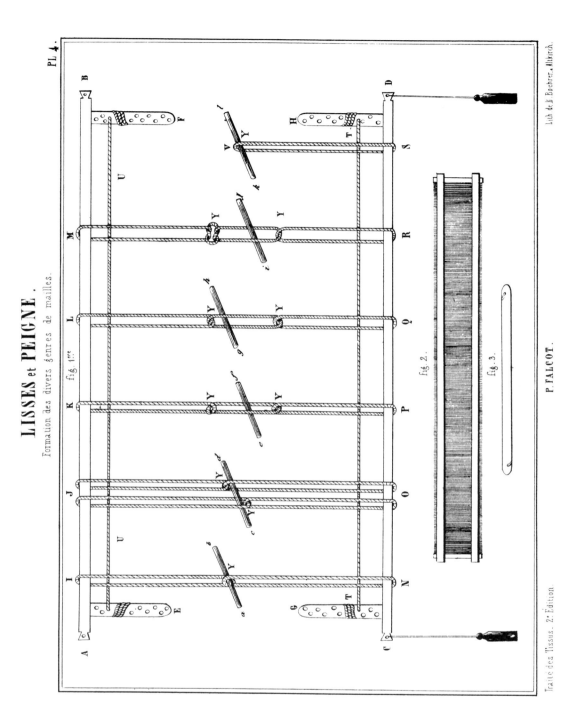

Plate 4 shows a variety of heddles mounted on a shaft – though any one shaft on a loom would have only one kind of heddle on it. I–N is the simplest and most economical, but liable to snap the thread (the illustrator has made a mistake here – the heddle should be 'clasped'). K–P, L–Q, M–R all show various ways of knotting to form a large loop, with the advantage of reducing wear in the warp threads. V–S is a half heddle attached to the bottom of the shaft, and used for *tissus à jour*. Cords T–T hold the heddles in place; their position can be varied to help prevent wear. They are used mainly in silk weaving.

The reed is the most important tool in obtaining a perfect fabric – the least imperfection could leave an irreparable flaw. It was originally made of natural reed, held in place by threads wound round the supports.

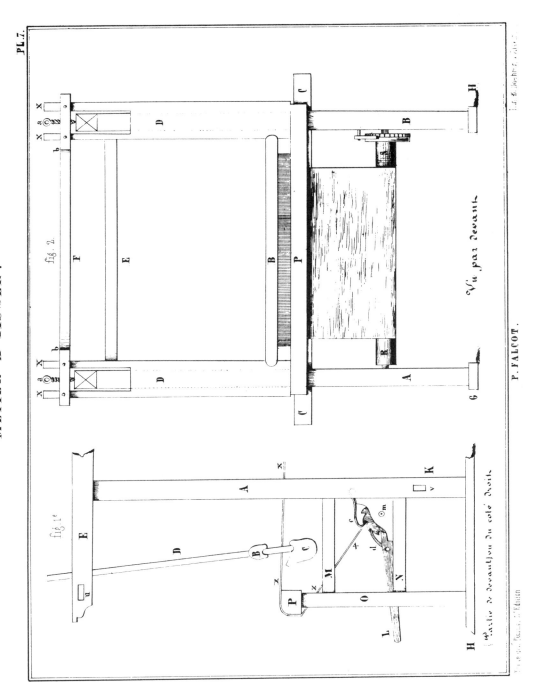

Plate 7 shows the use of a breast-beam, the woven fabric being wound on to the front beam which is mounted at knee height with a ratchet for winding on (see Plate 10). This arrangement is most generally used for fabrics where the thickness of a build-up of cloth on the front roller is likely to prove a problem – such as hangings, carpets, rugs, etc. The breast-beam can be replaced by a cylindrical roller; the former gives a certain amount of friction to the fabric, which may be desirable in the case of satins but is sometimes not wanted – the weaver must choose which is appropriate.

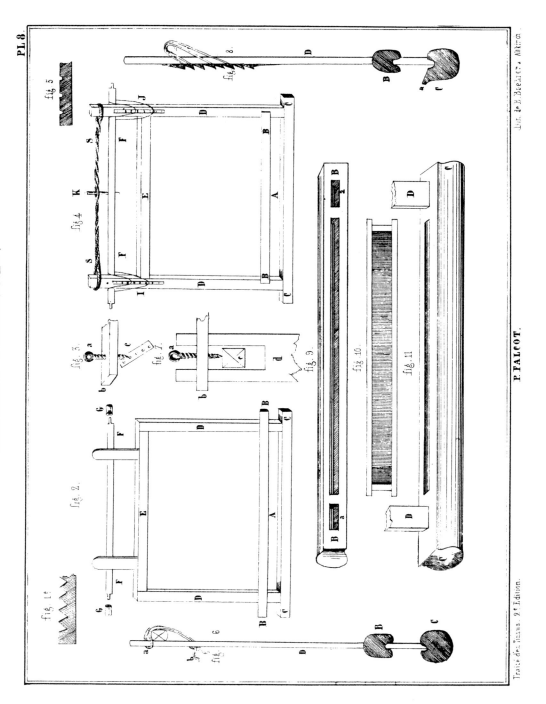

Plate 8 shows the basic batten. This supports the reed and beats the weft against the cloth. It is important that its weight is correct for the cloth being woven; extra weight can be added by fixing a metal bar to the back of the base.

The batten cap can be either supported by mortices B–B (fig.2) or forked at the end and screwed or pegged down B–B (fig.4). Fig.6 shows the side view of a simple fixing to the upright, with a cord passed over the traverse and knotted through a hole (b). Fig.8 shows a more elaborate fixing, with a looped cord hooked into a notched panel, allowing for the height of the batten to be varied (though Falcot prefers the system of wooden screws shown in Plate 9).

The batten rests on the loom frame by means of pegs; a method of adjustable support is shown in fig.3, where screw tips rest in holes. K, a twisted cord as shown in fig.4, helps to hold the batten firm.

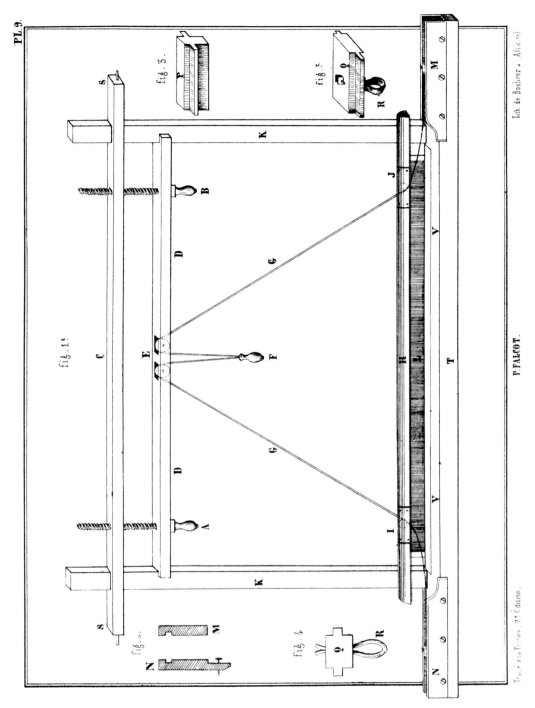

BATTANT A BOITES SIMPLES.

Plate 9 shows a simple flying shuttle batten, with one box at each end. The pickers (fig.3) fit in the boxes M and N and have a cord attached which runs through pulleys to the handle F; pulling this cord moves the pickers with sufficient impetus to propel the shuttle across the batten. For heavier work, a cord from each picker can be held, one in each hand.

The flying shuttle is recommended for direct and rapid movement of the shuttle; it is best for wide cloth and cheaper fabrics which need to be woven faster.

For fine fabrics, the front of the batten needs to be of hard wood kept well polished; a rod of polished iron or, better, glass, can be fixed behind the reed to help the warp slide through.

ROULEAUX ET OREILLONS.

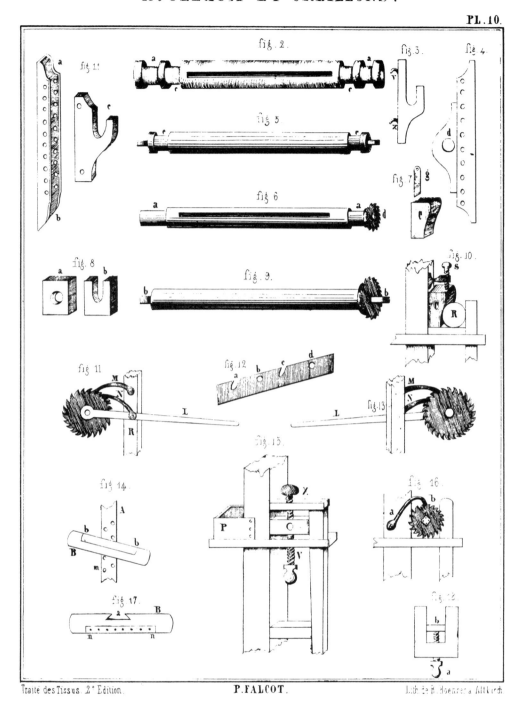

Traité des Tissus. 2ᵉ Edition.　　　P.FALCOT.　　　Lith de R.Hoennen a Altkirch.

Plate 10 shows beams and their supports. The back beam holds the warp, the front one the woven fabric. They can be held either in sockets or by pegs (fig.8). Back beams have two additional side grooves to hold the tensioning cord or cords. Longitudinal grooves hold the rod with the warp end (see Plate 3). The front beam always has an iron ratchet (fig.16). Generally, beams supported by pins are preferable to those supported in sockets.

Figs 14 and 17 show methods of attaching and adjusting the weaver's seat to the side of the loom – comfort is important when working.

Figs 11 and 13 show the ratchet for the breast-beam – the top pin (M) retains the tension, the bottom one holds the beam.

Several rollers at once could be mounted at the back using the mounting shown in fig.12.

Plate 11 shows a variety of shuttles, to be used according to the type of fabric.

The curved shuttles are for hand throwing; straight ones for the flying shuttle. Both can

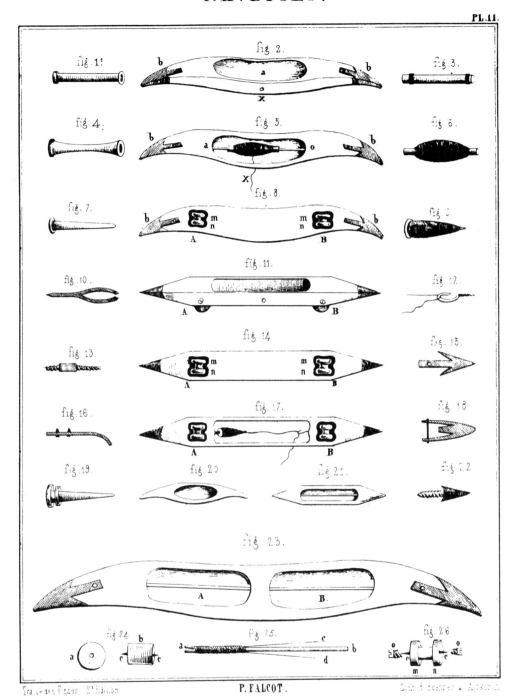

fig.1. fig.2. fig.3.

fig.4. fig.5. fig.6.

fig.7. fig.8. fig.9.

fig.10. fig.11. fig.12.

fig.13. fig.14. fig.15.

fig.16. fig.17. fig.18.

fig.19. fig.20. fig.21. fig.22.

fig.23.

fig.24. fig.25. fig.26.

P. FALCOT.

be used with or without rollers and vary in size and weight according to the fabric; the rollers are slightly larger on one side than the other to allow for the throwing curve (fig.24b). Metal tips can be a plate over the end (figs. 15 and 18) or a cone (fig.22). Shuttles need to be absolutely smooth to avoid snagging threads.

Hand shuttles are curved to avoid damaging the reed as they pass in front of it; the bottoms are hollowed out to reduce friction on the warp.

Flying shuttles need to be heavy enough not to deviate as they cross the fabric. The thread passes through a glass-lined hole.

Bobbins for both types of shuttle either unroll or unwind. There are several kinds of bobbin for unrolling (figs. 1, 3 and 4) – the latter is used when the thread is unstable. They are held in place by a whalebone pin (fig.25) fixed in the shuttle, which holds them under friction from the pins (c and d). Unwinding bobbins are fixed on a screw or forked peg; the thread unwinds over a hook. Double shuttles are also available, taking two bobbins at once.

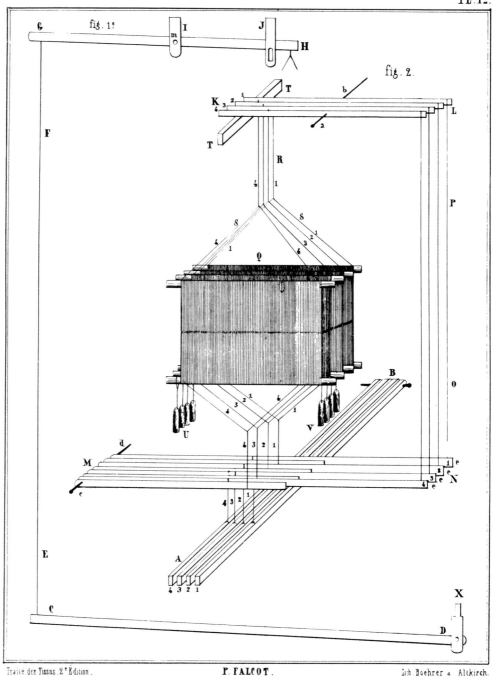

Traite des Tissus. 2ᵉ Édition.

P. FALCOT.

Lith. Boehrer à Altkirch.

Plate 12 The diagram (fig.2) shows the system of pedals and levers of a counterweighted loom. The shafts are weighted, and lifted to make a shed by means of the pedals.

Note that the operating cords O–P pass at the side of the loom, avoiding the middle of the warp.

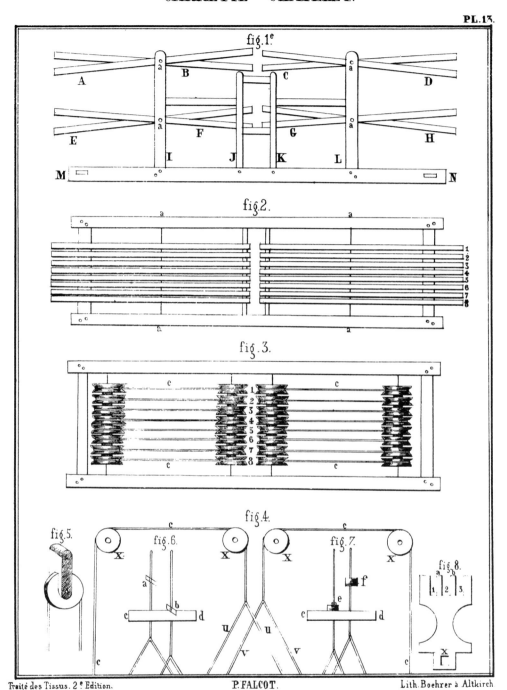

fig.1e

fig.2.

fig.3.

fig.4.

fig.5.

fig.6.

fig.7.

fig.8.

Traité des Tissus. 2.e Edition.   P. FALCOT.   Lith. Boehrer à Altkirch.

Plate 13 shows the mechanism, mounted on the top of the loom, by which the pedals and lams operate to raise and lower the shafts. Fig.1 shows in its entirety a possible two-deck system for use with a large number of shafts; more usually however, there is either the double-sided mounting E–F, G–H or the single G–H mounted at one side of the loom. Fig.1 is the elevation, fig.2 the plan. Fig.3 shows the plan where jacks have been replaced by pulleys; this has the advantage of raising the shafts in a straighter line, instead of a curve, and they do not have to be so high. In this case, the shafts are maintained at a regular level by means of small stoppers (e–f in fig.7).

TENSION DES CHAÎNES. — BASCULES DIVERSES.

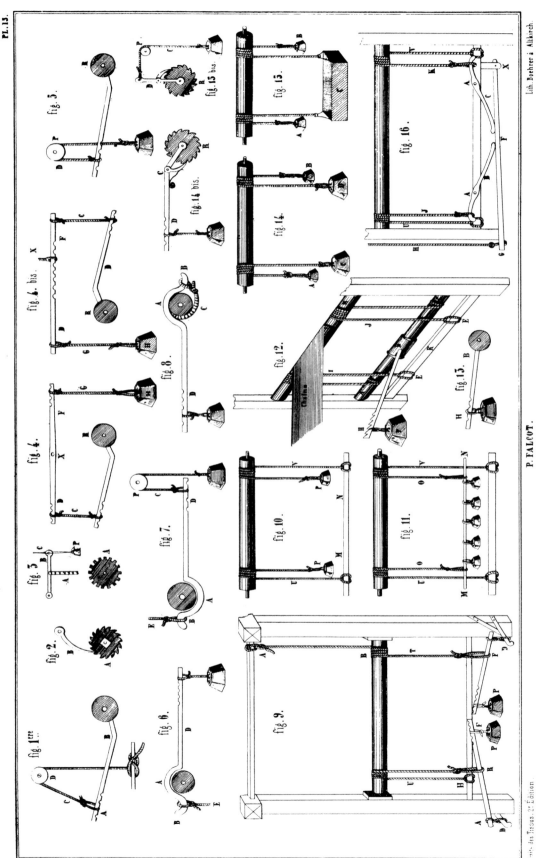

P. FALCOT.

Lith. Boehrer à Altkirch.

Plate 15 shows various ways of maintaining the warp in a proper tension, which varies according to the type of fabric being woven. Whether tight or loose, it needs to be constant. 'Getting the right tension is a science involving knowledge of the mechanics of the loom, as well as the yarns and the weaving methods to be used.' Tensioning is either fixed, mobile or retrograde. Fixed tensioning is the most basic, and generally not recommended (figs. 1, 2 and 3); it is impossible to regulate precisely, and can cause imperfections in the weave.

Various methods of mobile tensioning are shown: weighted beams, counterbalanced or friction balanced. Fig.12 shows 'the most modern and elegant method' – a weight held on a lever fixed in a slotted beam.

Fig.16 shows a method where levers B–C are held in tension by the long lever F, held on the cord H which is governed from the front of the loom.

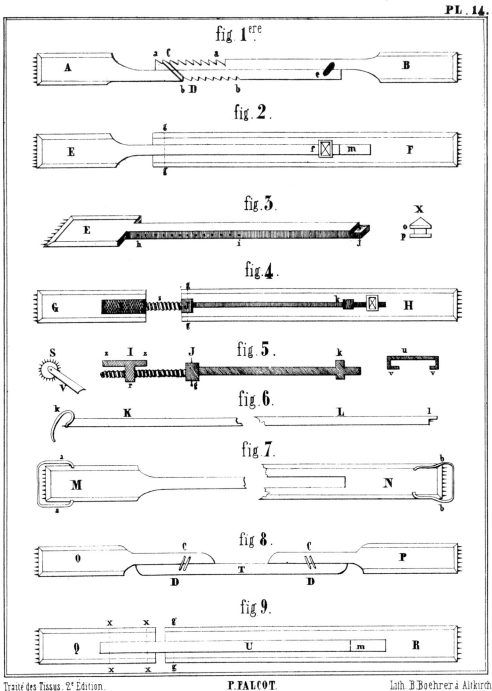

fig. 1ère.

fig. 2.

fig. 3.

fig. 4.

fig. 5.

fig. 6.

fig. 7.

fig 8.

fig 9.

Traité des Tissus. 2ᵉ Édition.   P. FALCOT.   Lith. B. Boehrer à Altkirch.

Plate 14 shows various kinds of temple which are used for maintaining the cloth at a regular width as it is woven. They can be adjusted by cords in grooves (fig.1), by a sliding adjustment and pin (figs. 2 and 3) or by a screw (figs. 4 and 5), this latter being preferable as it is more precise.

The pins at the ends vary in thickness and number according to the fabric to be used. They can be covered, to avoid injury to the weaver, by a piece of leather, a metal band or preferably by an overhang of the temple end – the safest and most generally adopted method.

Temples are generally extendable by 15–20 cm, but this can be extended by an additional stick added between the two parts.

The temples are fixed in the selvedges, whose main function it is to hold them. For this reason, selvedges need to be strong, and are made of cheaper yarn than the fabric – important for silk, but even more so for wool where the finishing process also puts strain on the selvedges.

USTENSILES & ACCESSOIRES DIVERS.

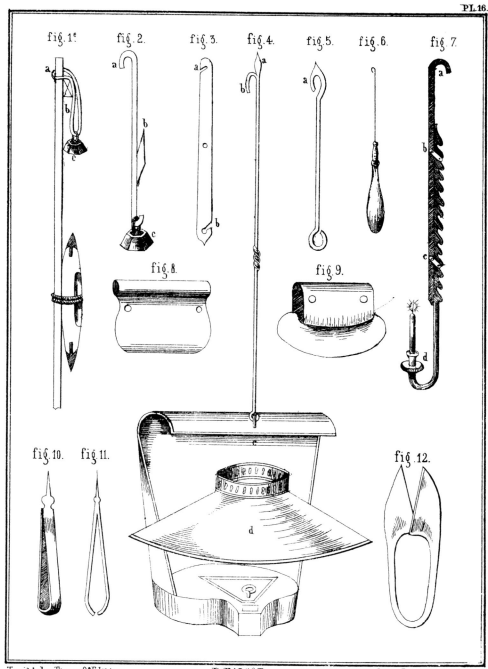

fig.1ᵉ. fig.2. fig.3. fig.4. fig.5. fig.6. fig.7.

fig.8. fig.9.

fig.10. fig.11. fig.12.

Traité des Tissus. 2ᵉ Edition. P. FALCOT. Lith. Boehrer à Altkirch.

Plate 16 shows various utensils and accessories. Figs. 3, 5 and 6 show threading hooks; 3 is a reed hook, 5 and 6 heddle hooks, though with cord heddles the weaver would thread with his fingers.

Snips (fig.12) are made of a single piece of metal; they are preferable to scissors as they can be operated in a single action and kept in the palm of the hand. *Pincettes* (figs. 10 and 11) are for removing flaws in the cloth or unravelling tangles in threads. Polishers (figs. 8 and 9) of metal or horn are used to remove the marks of the reed from some silk fabrics. Figs. 1 and 2 show the *valet* which holds the entered threads one by one until there are enough for a temporary tie.

(Falcot does not describe the lamps, which are a poignant reminder of the poor light in which much work must have been done, and the toll it took on eyesight.)

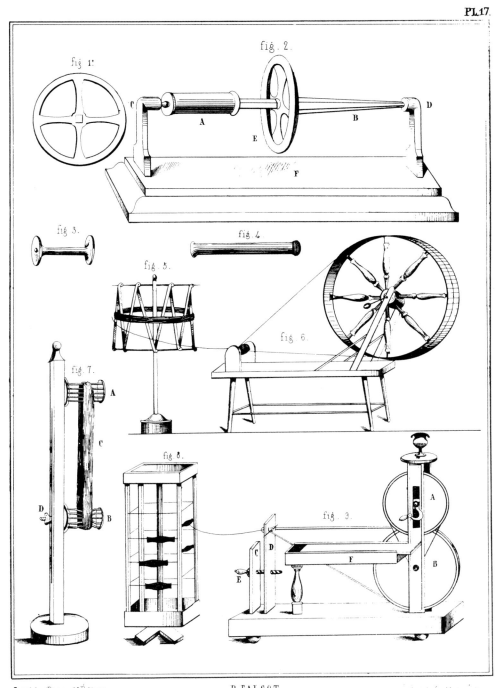

Plate 17 shows different ways of winding bobbins. A simple wheel and a swift are used for heavy yarns (figs. 5 and 6). Another simple winder is shown at fig.2; it is compact and can be used on the knee, but it is slow.

A fast winder (fig.9) is used for fine yarns, especially silk. There are also mechanical bobbin-winders, not shown, which will make several bobbins at once.

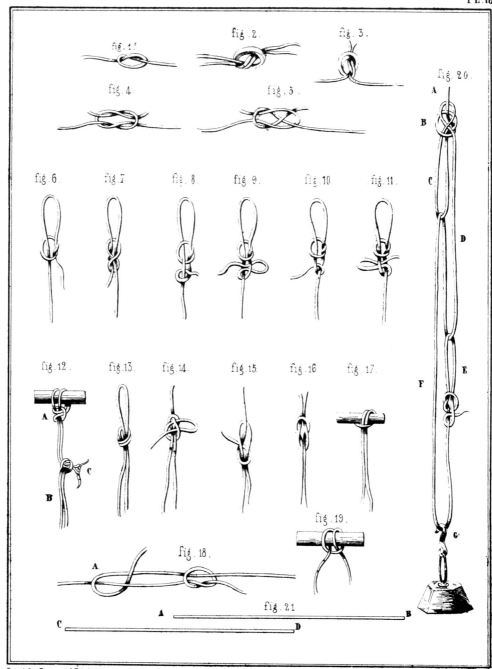

Traité des Tissus, 2ᵉ Édition.   P. FALCOT.   Lith. de Boehrer à Altkirch.

Plate 18 A good repertoire of knots is important; just one poor knot which fails can cause much extra work to repair the damage. Some of the principal knots of use to the weaver are shown here.

Simple knot (figs. 1, 2 and 3), either single or double.

Flat knot (reef knot) (4) and weaver's knot or fingernail knot (5), both firm and unbulky, the latter used in making simple heddles.

Slip knot (6 and 7) – a simple knot with the end threaded through; (8) slip knot fixed with secondary half-knot; (9) the same, with quick-release end. Stopping knot (snitch knot) (12c).

Buckle knot (10 and 11) – same as the stopping knot but used when there is only a single cord.

Collar knot (lark's head knot) (12A), used for attaching to shafts. It holds firm but is not too hard to untie. Simple collar knot (17) is not recommended – too flimsy.

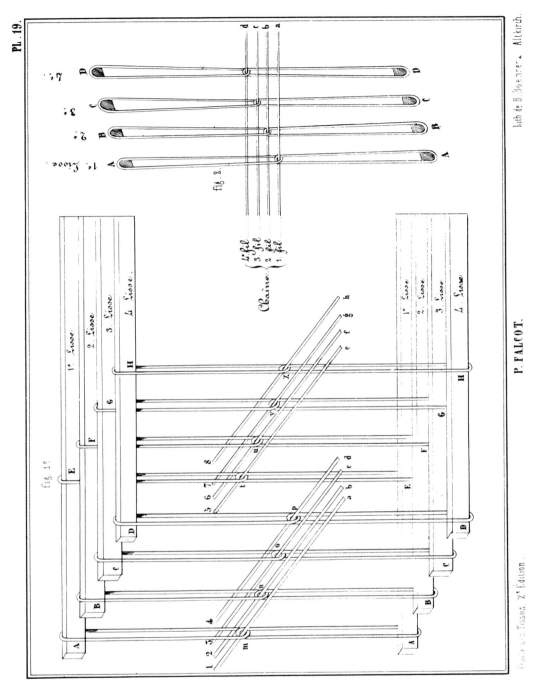

Pulling knot (18), used to join two broken ends – the thread is passed through the flat knot which is tensioned and then held by the half-knot A.

Fig.20 'as ingenious as it is useful' – an adjustable combination of several knots, which needs to be in constant tension.

Plate 19 shows the threading of the heddles. Although the weaver could do this himself it was quicker and cheaper to get expert threaders in, one to thread and another to pass the threads. 'Threading needs more patience and concentration than talent.'

Shafts and heddles need to be well set and correctly positioned before starting. Except for straight threading, a draft needs to be worked out beforehand. The back left-hand shaft is always the starting point. Threaded heddles are held by a *valet*, until there are enough to make a temporary tie (see Plate 16).

ROUET À RETORDRE.

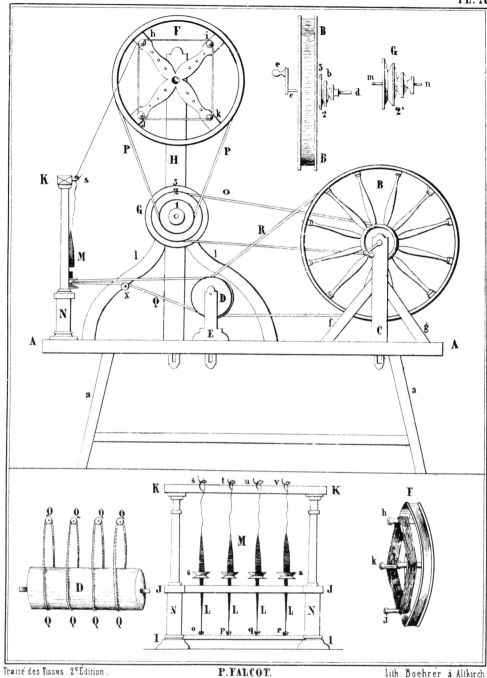

Traité des Tissus. 2ᵉ Édition.   **P. FALCOT.**   Lith. Boehrer à Altkirch.

Plate 28 shows how to ply threads, necessary for the warp. The master wheel (B), mounted on the table (A), turns by a system of cords, the bobbins mounted in the rack (K), and the winding wheel (F) where the hank of plied thread is held on pegs h, i, j, and k. As these are 25cm apart, each turn gives one metre of yarn. The length of plied yarn will be less than the singles from which it is made, by how much depends on the tightness of the twist. Twist can be either to the left or the right. (Falcot argues for a standardized terminology to avoid confusion – he would have approved of the S and Z description we use today.)

Twist is adjusted by the gearing of the wheels, done by moving the cords on to larger or smaller grooves on the hub of the wheel (B) or the pulley (G). A slow turning of the wheel (F) gives a tighter twist.

The small version shown would not be practical for long lengths, but is ideal for workshops producing samples.

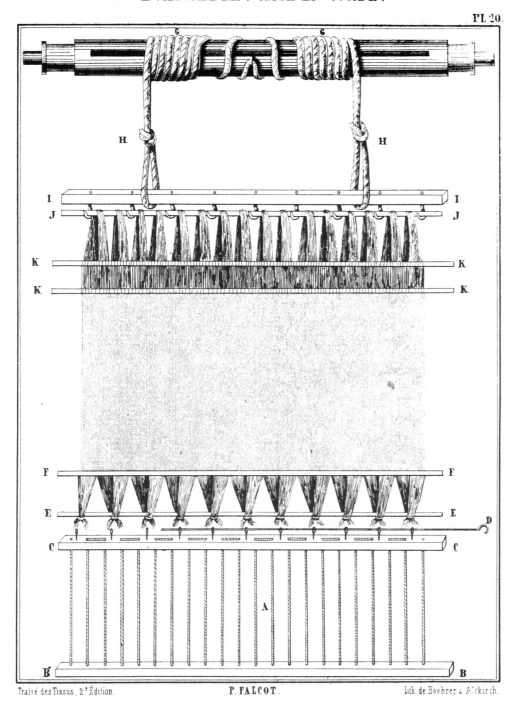

Traité des Tissus, 2ᵉ Édition.　　　P. FALCOT.　　　Lith. de Boehrer à Altkirch.

Plate 20 shows methods of tying on the warp at the front (B, C, D and E) and at the back (H, I and J) in order to give additional length and thus minimize the waste incurred by attaching the warp directly to the beams. At the front there are two wooden rods (B and C), joined by a cord; the piece (B) fits into the groove in the front beam, the warp is joined to the rod (D) which passes through eyelets; or it can be laced directly on to the rod (C).

At the back, a cord (H) ties round the warp beam and holds a bar (I) on to which is hung the rod (J) holding the back of the warp. In all cases, care must be taken to keep the tension even.

The principle is the same as that of attaching a cloth apron to the front and back beams. In fact, Falcot notes approvingly the use of a cloth as an alternative to the cords at A, which have the disadvantage of being liable to leave an impression on the weaving as it is wound on.

24

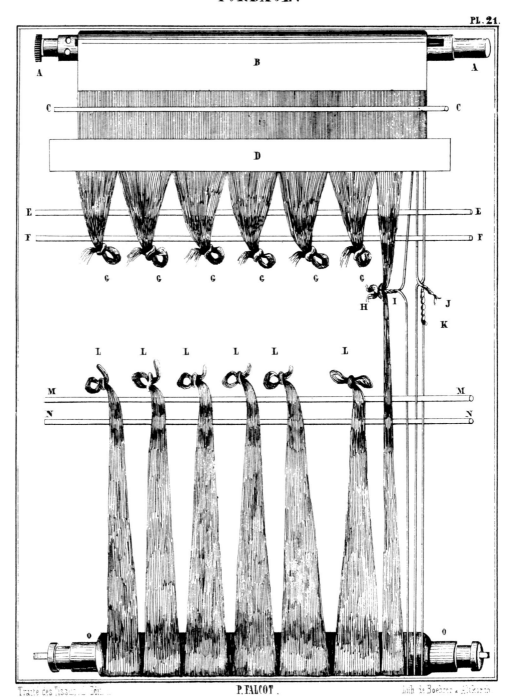

Traité des Tissus. Pl. ..   P. FALCOT .   Lith. de Boehrer & Altaran

Plate 21 shows the twisting-in of a new warp on to the end of a previous one. It will be seen that the threads of both old and new warps have been tied loosely into bundles, and that threads are pulled one at a time from each one and joined together. This method is suitable for silk.

PAPIERS RÉGLES.

pour la mise en carte des cartons.

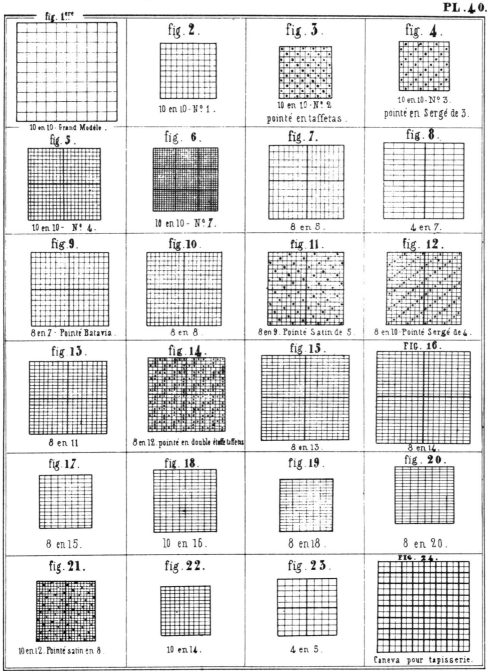

fig. 1ère	fig. 2.	fig. 3.	fig. 4.
10 en 10. Grand Modéle.	10 en 10 - N° 1.	10 en 10 - N° 2. pointé en taffetas.	10 en 10 - N° 3. pointé en Sergé de 3.
fig. 5.	fig. 6.	fig. 7.	fig. 8.
10 en 10 - N° 4.	10 en 10 - N° 7.	8 en 5.	4 en 7.
fig. 9.	fig. 10.	fig. 11.	fig. 12.
8 en 7 - Pointé Batavia.	8 en 8.	8 en 9. Pointé Satin de 5.	8 en 10 - Pointé Sergé de 4.
fig. 13.	fig. 14.	fig. 15.	FIG. 16.
8 en 11	8 en 12. pointé en double étoffe taffetas	8 en 13.	8 en 14.
fig. 17.	fig. 18.	fig. 19.	fig. 20.
8 en 15.	10 en 16.	8 en 18.	8 en 20.
fig. 21.	fig. 22.	fig. 23.	FIG. 24.
10 en 12. Pointé satin en 8.	10 en 14.	4 en 5.	Caneva pour tapisserie.

Traité des Tissus. 2ᵉ Édition.   **P. FALCOT.**   Lith. Boehrer à Altkirch.

Plate 40 shows various ruled papers for drafting and analysis. In early drafts lines were drawn to represent warp and weft, with the line itself representing the thread, but it became more practical to use squared paper, with the spaces representing the threads, and a conventional system of marks. The divisions of the squares into different proportions is to allow for the representation of designs for fabric, which is either warp- or weft-faced, without distortion.

The ability to analyse fabric is useful, as it allows the weaver to reproduce fashionable fabrics quickly. Sometimes analysis can be made by eye, but with fine threads a count-glass is needed. When undoing fabric, it is necessary to establish warp and weft, and to write down the notation thread by thread. Several repeats should be unravelled to be sure of getting the pattern right. If a sample cannot be unravelled for some reason it may not be possible to produce a perfect copy.

This plate shows several possible grids for analysis, some of which have been completed as examples.

SYSTÈME LÈVE-BAISSE.

Métier à la marche.

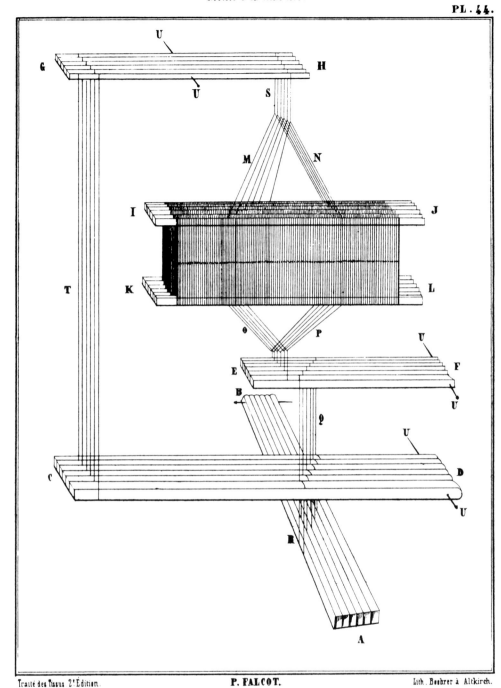

Traité des Tissus 2ᵉ Édition. P. FALCOT. Lith. Boehrer à Altkirch.

Plate 44 illustrates the system of pedals and levers for a countermarch loom, with rising and falling shed. (The illustrator has made several mistakes in the relation of cords to rails.)

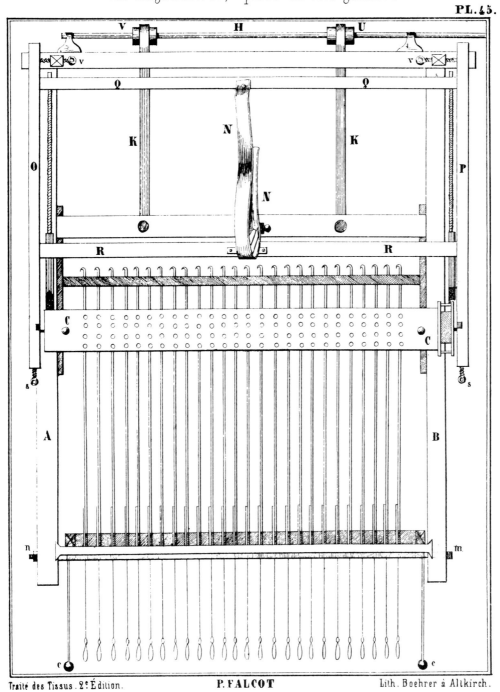

Traité des Tissus. 2ᵉ Édition.   P. FALCOT   Lith. Boehrer à Altkirch.

Plate 45 shows the side of the mechanism with the *planchette* (C). This is the board against which the cylinder with pattern cards presses, the needles slipping into the holes in the board corresponding with the holes in the pattern cards.

MÉCANIQUE ARMURE.

Vue longitudinale, prise du coté droit.

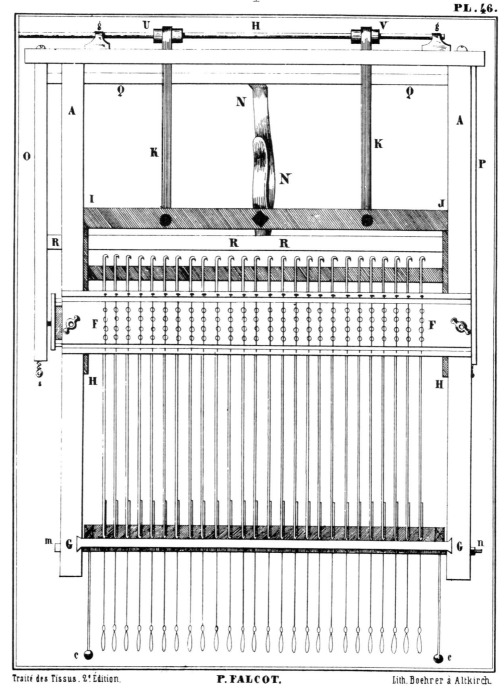

Traité des Tissus. 2.e Édition.   **P. FALCOT.**   Lith. Boehrer à Altkirch.

Plate 46 shows the other side, and the needlecase (F) with the holes into which the needles are pushed by meeting the cylinder with an unpunched card. The pins retaining the springs in each hole can be seen clearly.

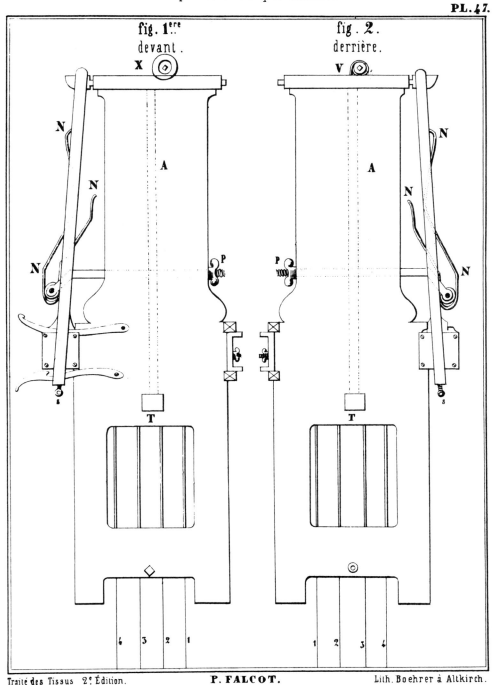

MÉCANIQUE ARMURE.
Vue par devant et par derrière.

fig. 1ère
devant.

fig. 2.
derrière.

X

V

N

N

N

N

A

A

N

N

P

P

N

N

T

T

4 3 2 1

1 2 3 4

Traité des Tissus 2ᵉ Édition.   P. FALCOT.   Lith. Boehrer à Altkirch.

Plate 47 shows front and back view, with the cylinder at rest against the frame.

Falcot recommends that the best way of using these looms is to thread up only one row of hooks and needles, which would give twenty-six shafts (about the maximum we would use today for a handloom).

MÉCANIQUE ARMURE.
Coupe transversale.

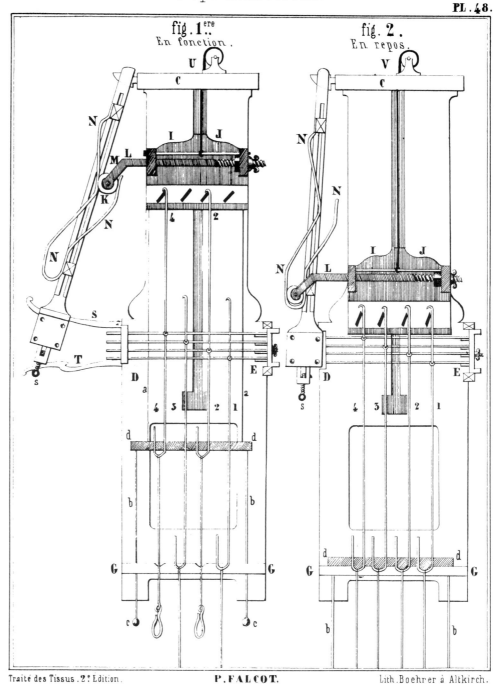

30

PL.48.

fig.1ère
En fonction.

fig.2.
En repos.

Traité des Tissus. 2ᵉ Édition.   P. FALCOT.   Lith. Boehrer à Altkirch.

Plate 48 The pattern cards pass one at a time over the cylinder, which is supported by its ratchets (S and T), which move it either forwards or in reverse. The cylinder moves against the needles, and where a needle encounters a hole it stays in position and is lifted with the griffe. When there is no hole the needle is pushed back into the needlecase against the spring, moving its hook which is displaced from the lifting mechanism, so no shaft lift takes place.

The movement of the mechanism is shown in Plate 48. (Fig.1 is inaccurate as it shows lifting of the shafts although the cylinder is not pressed against the needles – presumably it has been drawn just to show the moving parts of the mechanism.)

The cylinder is turned by the metal spring (N); as the griffe moves up, the roller (L) attached to it pushes the beater out, and the metal latches (S and T) advance or reverse the cylinder by one turn.

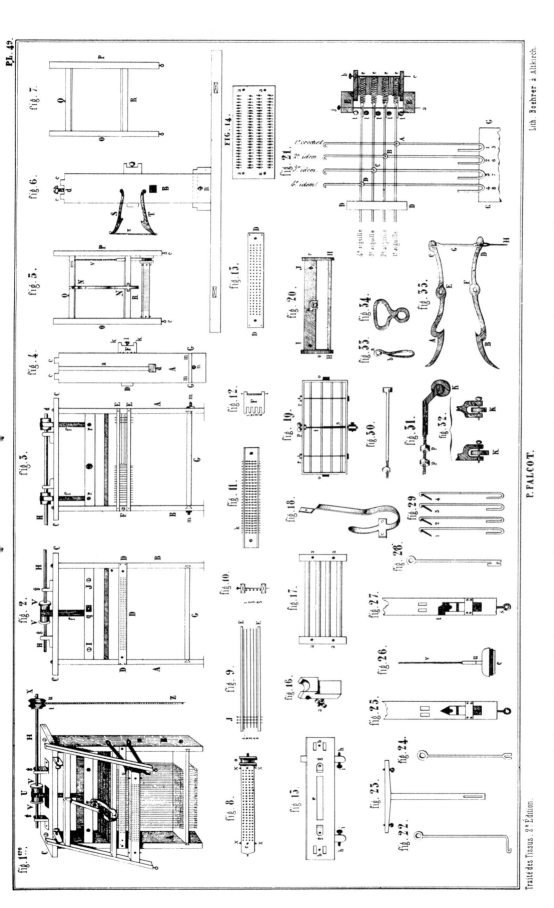

Traité des Tissus. 2ᵉ Édition.

P. FALCOT.

Lith. Boehrer à Altkirch.

Plate 49 shows a small Jacquard mechanism dismantled to show its composition, and a perspective view (fig.1). This is a variation of the Jacquard principle suitable mainly for small-scale designs, using shafts only (up to 104, although only twenty-six were normally used). The mechanism is mounted in a frame (fig.1) which is fixed above the loom longitudinally with the cylinder for feeding the pattern cards at the left (as shown in profile in Plate 47).

Fig.21 shows in detail the arrangements of needles and hooks. Each hook lifts a shaft. Both the *planchette* (D) and the needlecase (E) have four rows of twenty-six holes. Each of the holes in the needlecase contains a brass spring which returns the needle to its place. Each needle is attached to a hook, and all the hooks rest in grooves on a collar-board or grate. The neck cords, which support the shafts, pass through holes in the grate, each hook being attached by one cord to one shaft.

The tops of the needles are hooked over the lifting mechanism, known as the griffe (fig.19) which consists of four flat metal bars placed at an angle (fig.29). As the griffe is raised, it carries the hooks, with it, unless they have been displaced by the pattern card.

MATRICE et PERÇAGE des CARTONS
par rang longitudinal pour la Mécanique   Armure.

PL.50

32

fig. 1ere

fig. 2.

fig. 3.   fig. 4.

fig. 5.

fig. 6.

fig. 7.

fig. 8.

fig. 9.

fig. 10.

fig. 11.

Traité des Tissus. 2.e Édition.   P. FALCOT.   Lith. Boehrer à Altkirch.

Plate 50 shows the method of punching cards using a mallet and two punches; a small one for the pattern, a large one for the locating holes. There is a metal matrix on a wooden base, on which the card is placed with a second matrix fitting over the top (fig.8). Each hole in a card representing a lift of a shaft matches a marked square on the weave draft. If only one row of hooks is used, it should be one of the middle ones; if two, they should be balanced (figs. 9, 10 and 11).

A ruler can be used to mark the place on the draft (fig.1). Right-handed people will punch from the left, left-handers the other way, to avoid the hand covering work already done. (The piano card cutter replaced this system.)

MÉCANIQUE ARMURE.
Perçage des Cartons par rang transversal.

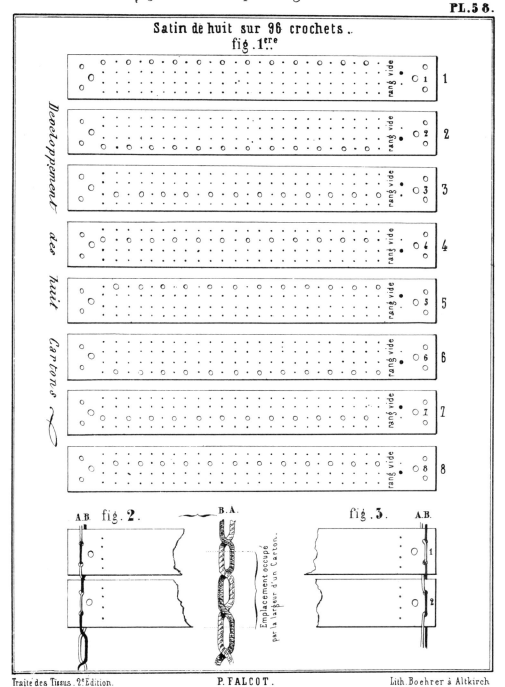

Satin de huit sur 96 crochets.
fig. 1ᵉʳᵉ

Plate 58 shows (fig.1) an example of a set of punched cards – for satin an eight-shaft design, shown on the first two short rows of four holes, and repeated across the card twelve times to give a ninety-six-shaft threading.

Also shown (fig.2) is the correct way of lacing a set of cards together. Two cords are used, and care should be taken to lace them in a consistent manner. If laced in a disorderly way (fig.3), the cards could twist and distort.

If only four cards are used, they can be tied directly on to the cylinder. A set of cards for a design is called a design, or a muff.

PIÈCES DÉTACHÉES
des Mécaniques dites à Tambour et à Planchettes.

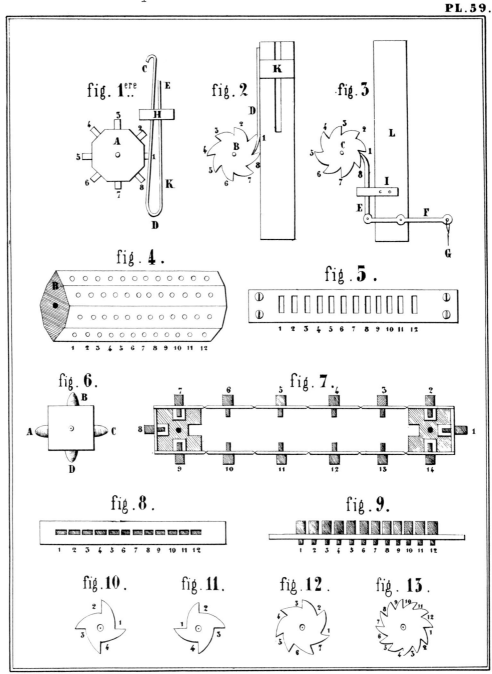

Traité des Tissus. 2ᵉ Edition.   **P. FALCOT.**   Lith. Boehrer à Altkirch.

Plate 59 shows two variations on the card-and-cylinder system.

One is the drum, whereby the cylinder is replaced by a drum with holes for pegs (figs. 1 and 4) which can be moved forward or back. There are no cards, the draft is pegged directly on to the drum. In this system, the pegs displace the hooks and leave their corresponding shafts at rest, so a blank on the draft, and therefore the drum, indicates a lifted shaft. This is a cheap system as there is no needle mechanism; however, there is a limit to the number of sides which a drum can have, so it is suitable only for simple designs.

The second version is the lag system (fig.7), where the drum is replaced by a cylinder with grooves and a set of wooden lags with holes. Each lag represents one lift; the draft is made with pegs in the lags. A longer draft can be used than with the drum system; however, the weight of the lags makes it hard to use the loom if there are more than about forty.

PRINCIPES d'EMPOUTAGES.

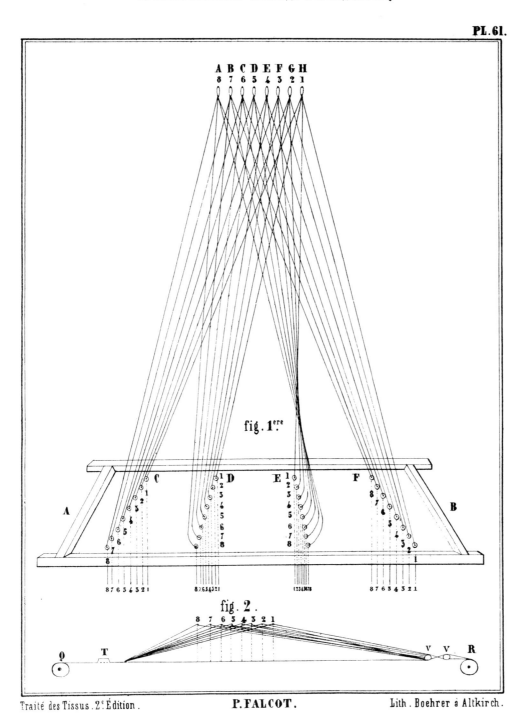

fig. 1.ere

fig. 2.

Traité des Tissus. 2.e Édition. **P. FALCOT.** Lith. Boehrer à Altkirch.

Plate 61 shows the principles for threading all the harness cords of the Jacquard loom through the comber board. It is not a complicated procedure, but needs to be done methodically, and in accordance with the requirements of the design.

Neck cords from the griffe (not shown) end at the loops A–H, and from them are threaded the harness cords, which then pass in sequence through the holes in the comber board; from each one hangs a weighted cord with an eyelet (the mail) through which the threads of the warp are threaded (see Plate 77). It will be seen that when the hook controlling A is raised, all the warp threads attached to it will rise. In this example there are four repeats across the design.

PLANCHES d'EMPOUTAGE.

Supports.── fausses-lisses ── faux-corps.

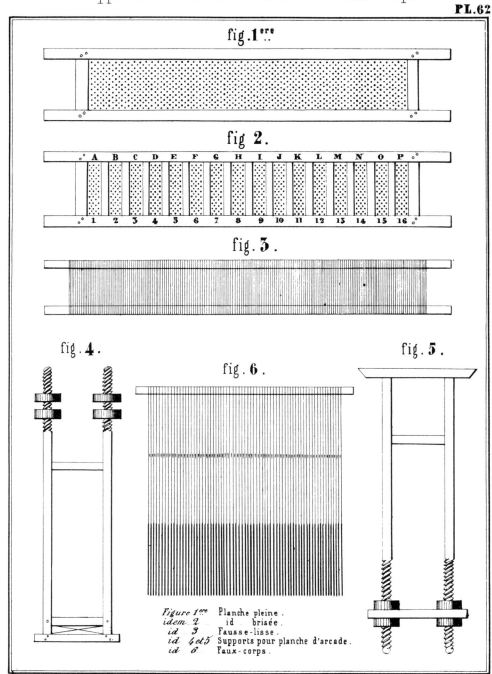

fig.1ere.

fig 2.

A B C D E F G H I J K L M N O P

1 2 3 4 5 6 7 8 9 10 11 12 13 14 15 16

fig. 3.

fig.4.

fig.6.

fig.5.

Figure 1ere Planche pleine.
idem 2   id   brisée.
id   3   Fausse-lisse.
id 4et5   Supports pour planche d'arcade.
id   6   Faux-corps.

Traité des Tissus. 2e Édition.   **P. FALCOT.**   Lith. Boehrer à Altkirch.

Plate 62 shows a standard comber board (fig.1), with the supports (figs. 4 and 5) which hold it while it is being threaded.

EMPOUTAGE SUIVI.

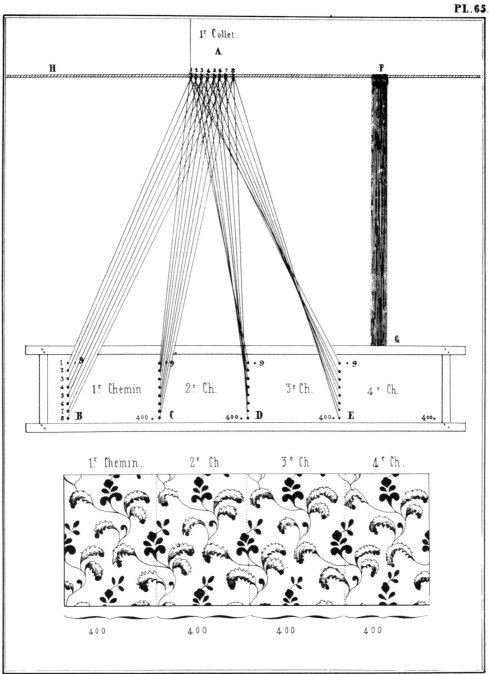

Traité des Tissus. 2.Édition **P. FALCOT.** Lith de Boehrer à Altkirch

Plate 65 shows the process of threading harness cords through the comber board. This takes place away from the loom. All the harness cords are hung at the right of a cord (H–F); the comber board is suspended horizontally in front of it. The threading sequence is worked out in advance, and it can be seen here that there is a straight repeat of 400 threads four times. The first eight threadings are shown in sequence, working from the back forwards.

If the full complement of cords is not being used, care must be taken that the empty spaces are left evenly; and the threading should extend over the full width of the fabric.

When threading is complete, the cords are tied loosely in groups, and the support cord (H–F) is tied. The whole assemblage is then taken to the loom for the next operation, the joining of harness cords to neck cords.

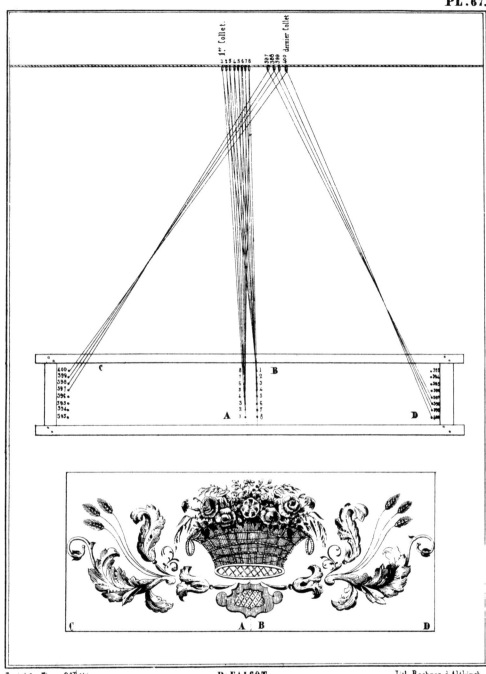

Traité des Tissus. 2.ᵉ Édition.   P. FALCOT.   Lith. Boehrer à Altkirch.

Plate 67 shows the arrangement for threading a design which is a mirror image – often used for furnishing fabric. The sequence of threading for this type of design starts in the middle, and can be followed from the diagram. For this kind of design it is best to use shafts for the background cloth, and the harness for the pattern.

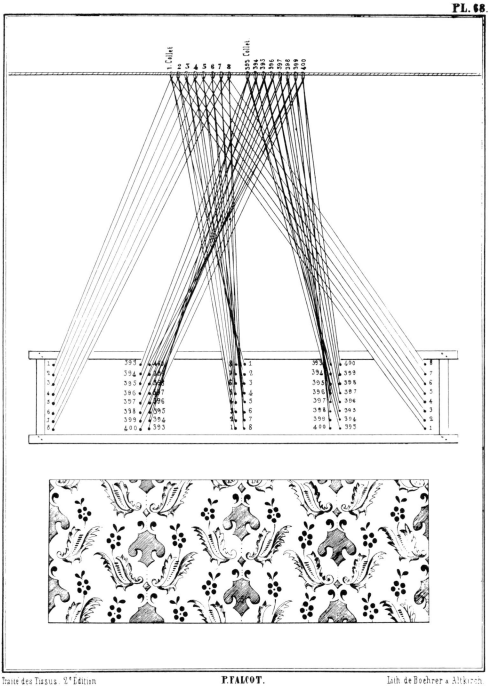

Traité des Tissus. 2ᵉ Édition   P. FALCOT.   Lith de Boehrer a Altkirch.

Plate 68 shows a repeat design like Plate 67, but on a smaller scale, and repeated four times across the fabric. The sequence of threading can be followed from the numbers shown. This kind of design can be used for a border, but is best as an all-over design, as shown at the foot of the plate.

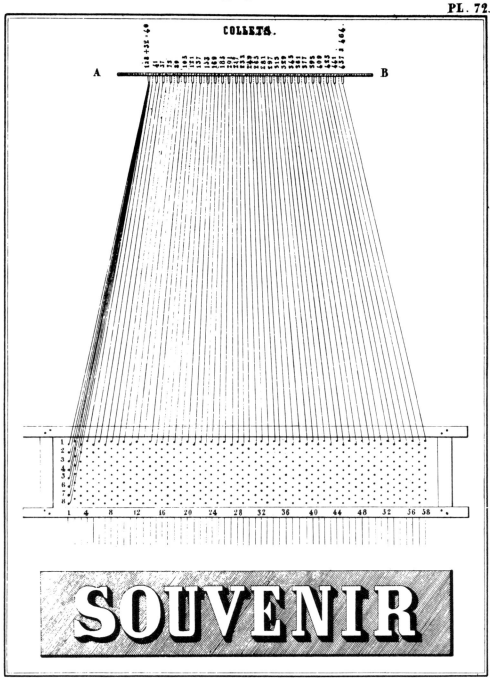

Traité des Tissus. 2.ᵉ Édition.　　　P. FALCOT.　　　Lith. Boehrer à Altkirch.

Plate 72 shows hybrid threading, made in a continuous sequence, where the design runs the full width of the fabric without repetition.

The background is threaded on the first five rows of the harness (forty cords), thereafter the threading of the motif is one thread to a harness cord, so the remaining 464 of the total 504 threads can be moved independently. This makes a thin fabric, as the number of warp threads is limited to the number in the harness. This can be alleviated, however, by putting more than one thread in each eyelet (see Plate 77) and adding shafts for the background.

PENDAGE. APPAREILLAGE.
Enverjure de Corps.

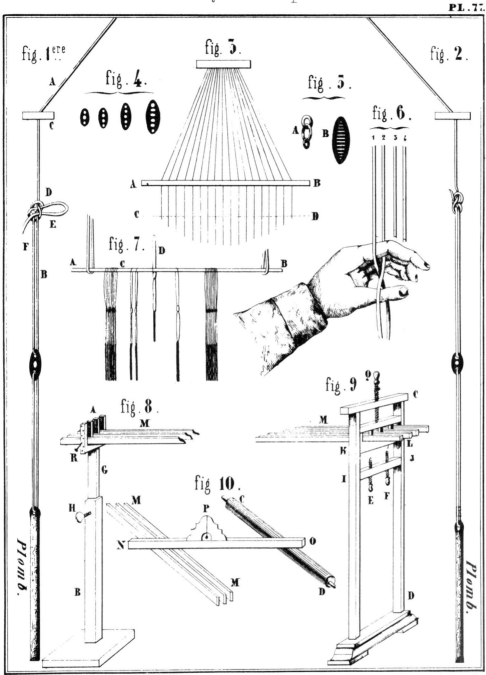

fig. 1ere. fig. 4. fig. 3. fig. 5. fig. 6. fig. 2.

fig. 7.

fig. 8. fig. 9. fig 10.

Traité des Tissus. 2e Édition.   P. FALCOT.   Lith. Boehrer à Altkirch.

Plate 77 shows some operations connected with the Jacquard harness. As can be seen in fig.3, the harness cords need to be straightened after they have been threaded through the comber board (A–B), before the mail cords are hung from them. The mails (figs. 4 and 5) are eyelets, made of glass or metal, with a minimum of three and a maximum of twelve holes; the top and bottom ones for hanging threads, the rest take the warp threads, as required. Each mail is held in tension by a weight, called a lingo (figs. 1 and 2).

Fig.7 shows the tying of mails to the harness cords by means of a guide rod. A temporary tie is made first, which is then fixed when all the cords are in place. Figs. 8 and 9 show devices used for holding the mail cords when the final tie is made.

The cross (fig.6) is worked straight across the back of the loom with finger and thumb; it is held on a thread while being made, and then held by sticks in the usual way, but vertically.

The eyelets are threaded with a *passette* (Plate 16); starting at the bottom if there is more than one thread in a mail.

ACCESSOIRES.

Signes conventionnels. — mise en carte

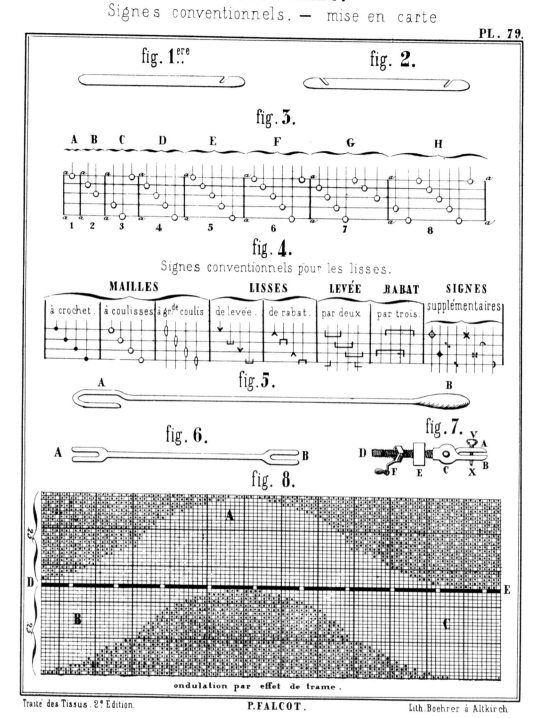

fig. 1.ᵉʳᵉ

fig. 2.

fig. 3.

A   B   C   D   E   F   G   H

1   2   3   4   5   6   7   8

fig. 4.

Signes conventionnels pour les lisses.

MAILLES			LISSES		LEVÉE	RABAT	SIGNES
à crochet.	à coulisses	à gr.ᵈᵉ coulis	de levée.	de rabat.	par deux	par trois.	supplémentaires

fig. 5.

A   B

fig. 6.

A   B

fig. 7.

D   F   E   C   X   B   A   V

fig. 8.

A

D   E

B   C

ondulation par effet de trame.

Plate 79 shows some more accessories. Figs. 1 and 2 are *passettes*, used when only one person is threading the reed; the thread is pushed through the reed which is suspended horizontally, from above.

Figs. 3 and 4 show the conventional notation for threading the reed when it is irregular (when regular, it can be indicated on the draft).

Figs. 5 and 7 show two devices used in the weaving of horsehair. Fig. 5 is a wooden stick with a glass or ivory hook which replaces the shuttle. A child at the side of the loom would put a horsehair weft thread into the hook, which would then be passed through the shed. Fig. 7 is a screw temple – an ordinary tenter will not work because the weft does not turn back on itself, so it will just pull out.

Fig. 6 is a *passerelle*, used for metallic threads instead of a shuttle. The threads are wound round the ends; the length of the bar is equal to the width of the weaving required.

CERCEAUX DIVERS.

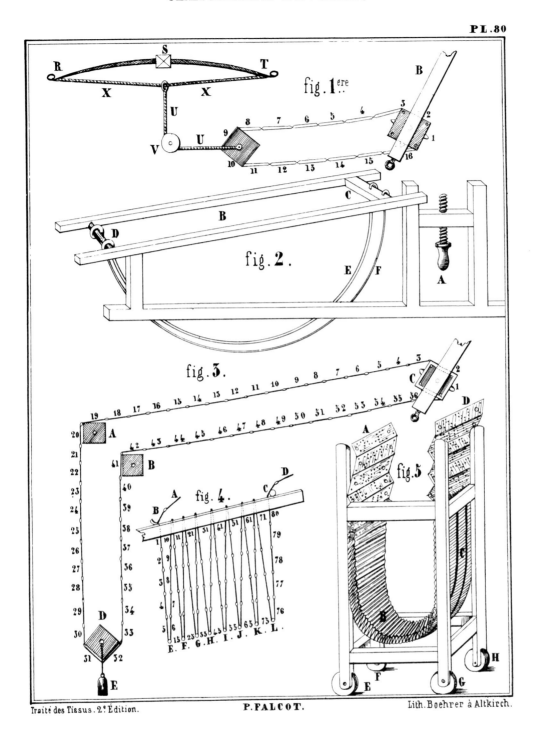

Traité des Tissus. 2ᵉ Édition.   P. FALCOT.   Lith.Boehrer à Altkirch.

Plate 80 shows various methods of holding the pattern cards on the loom either in tension as fig.1 or by hanging (fig.3). The supports can be a variety of shapes – a cradle is shown at fig.2.

With a large number of cards, a metal rod can be laced in at intervals, say every ten cards, which will suspend them in a rack, as at fig.4. This can cope with about 6,000 to 8,000 cards; but for a very large design, such as a shawl, 30,000 cards is not unusual, and then the cards are supported in a wooden rack (fig.5).

MÉTIER A LA JACQUARD.
Vu de Coté.

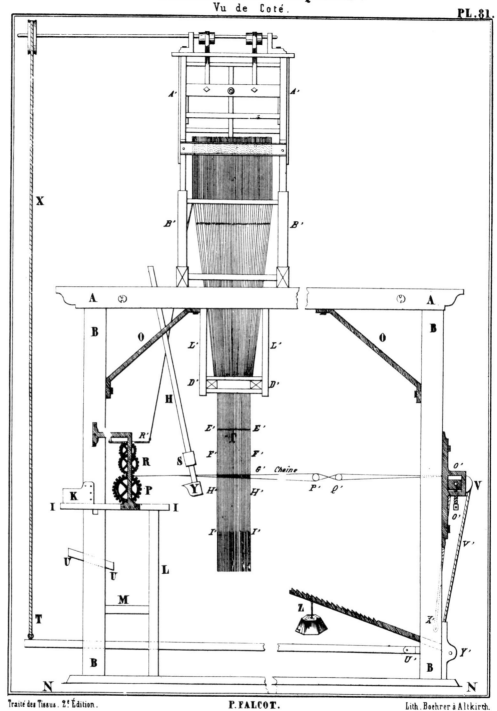

Traité des Tissus. 2.ᵉ Édition.   P. FALCOT.   Lith. Boehrer à Altkirch.

Plates 81 and 82 show the Jacquard loom itself. The mechanism works in the same way as the small Jacquard (Plates 45–49). The main difference is that the Jacquard mechanism enables warp threads to be raised independently. Instead of shafts, the warp threads are controlled by individual cords attached to the griffe (lifting device), which is controlled by the pattern cards.

The loom is made in several standard sizes, described according to the number of hooks the mechanism contains: 100, 200, 400, 600, 900, or 1,200 (the latter is not recommended as the weight of the harness can be too great for the loom which will buckle). Mechanisms can be combined. In practice, there are usually a few more hooks than the number quoted. Shafts are sometimes used as well; they are useful in providing the ground weave.

MÉTIER A LA JACQUARD.

Vu par devant .

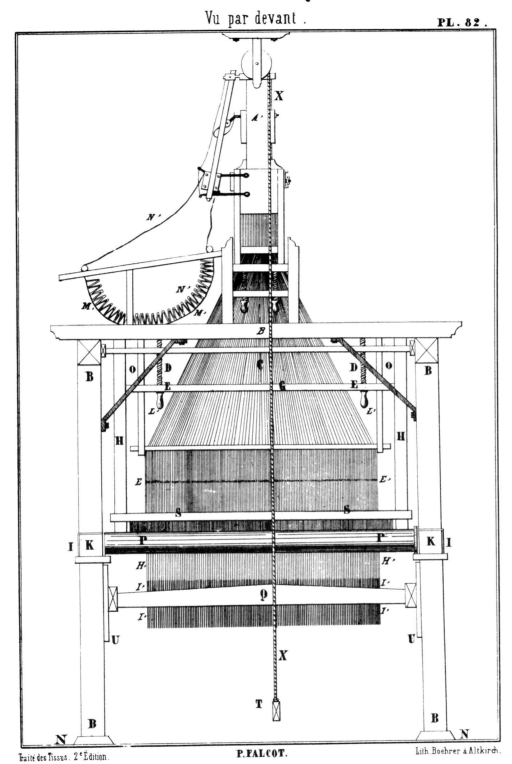

Traité des Tissus. 2ᵉ Édition.

P. FALCOT.

Lith. Boehrer à Altkirch.

Plate 82 shows clearly the arrangement of the harness – the harness cords fanning out from the neck board and passing through the comber board, and the mail cords weighted by their lingoes. The card support frame is also clearly shown, with the cards passing over the cylinder.

Jacquard is Falcot's hero – he devotes a chapter to the story of his life and invention. The loom mechanism is revolutionary, combining lightness, elegance, speed and the lightening of effort. Although it was derided and destroyed by those who feared losing their livelihood, when first introduced, by the mid-nineteenth century, when Falcot wrote, it had been accepted and was the foundation of the Lyons weaving trade.

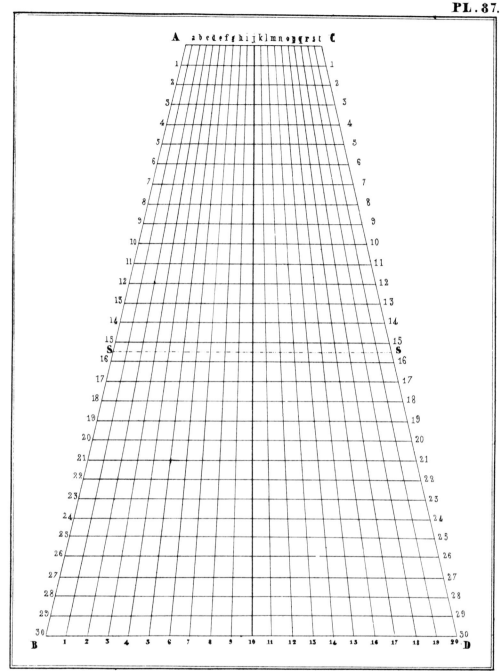

Traite des Tissus. 2.ᵉ Édition.   **P. FALCOT.**   Lith. de B.Boehrer à Altkirch.

Plate 87 shows the regulator, a grid used when the painted design, or *esquisse*, is to be transferred to point paper as a draft. The design is painted freehand, full size, and needs to be scaled down on to point paper. This regulator helps divide it into grids, which correspond to the grids of the point paper.

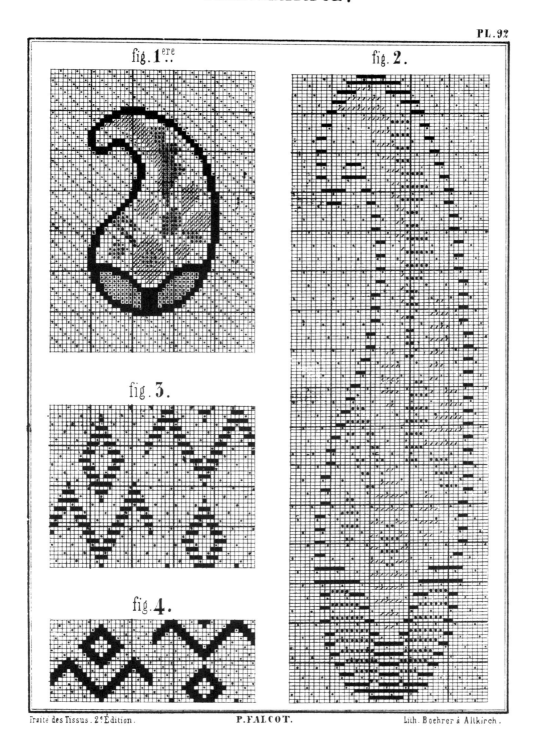

fig.1ere   fig.2.

fig.3.

fig.4.

Traité des Tissus. 2eÉdition.   P.FALCOT.   Lith. Boehrer à Altkirch.

Plate 92 In some cases a design may need more than one colour to a pick. Each row of the draft has to be separated by colour.

Fig.1 shows a design in three colours – black, red and green. This is translated in fig.2 to show just one colour for each pick. Naturally the design is distorted, as there are now two or more rows of the draft for each pick.

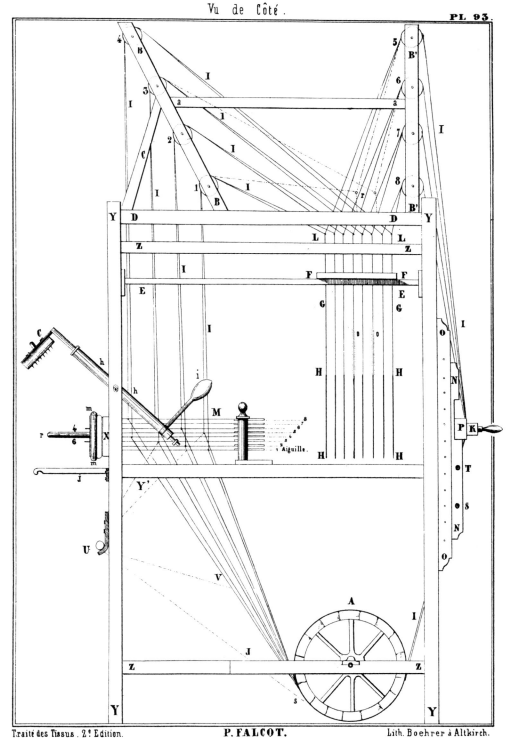

LISAGE À TAMBOUR.
Vu de Côté.

Traité des Tissus. 2ᵉ Edition.   P. FALCOT.   Lith. Boehrer à Altkirch.

Plates 93, 94 and 95 all show a machine used for turning the draft into a set of punch cards. The machine is used in conjunction with the punching table, and also a repeating machine for copying.

   Plate 93 shows the machine in profile: a framework with four rollers on each side and continuous cords which pass over them and round the large wheel at the bottom. The number of cords corresponds to the count of the loom to be used. On the back (right of the plate) is the mechanism for reading the draft, and on the front (left of the plate) is the mechanism for making a template of the draft, which is then taken to the punching table. A set of cords and needles can be seen arranged as on the Jacquard loom.

Traité des Tissus. 2ᵉ Édition. **P. FALCOT.** Lith. Boehrer à Altkirch.

Plate 94 shows the back of the machine, where the draft of the design is fixed. It is woven on cords (the simple) which are threaded round the machine. It can be seen at the bottom of the diagram that five picks have been woven, corresponding to the first five lines of the draft. These picks are made of short lengths of yarn, tied to cords at the side. Eventually a complete replica of the pattern is woven on the simple cords.

LISAGE À TAMBOUR
Côté du perçage.

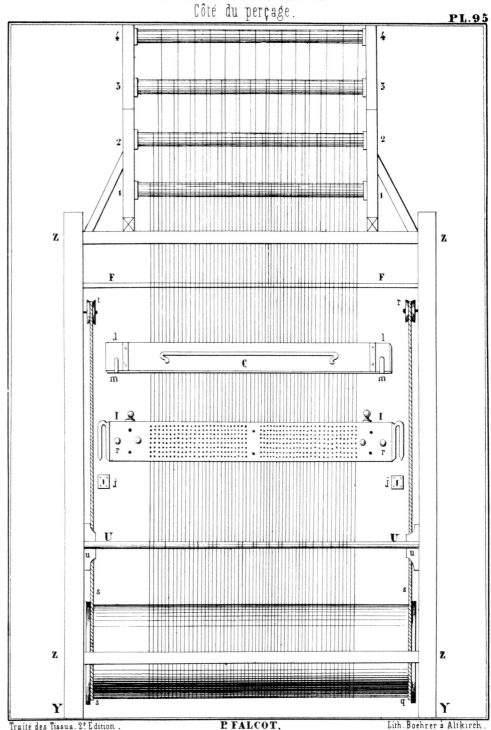

Traité des Tissus. 2ᵉ Édition.   **P. FALCOT.**   Lith. Boehrer à Altkirch.

Plate 95 shows the other side of the machine. The weave draft on its continuous cord is pulled through, under the wheel, and up to the level of the needlecase. This is made like the Jacquard box, except that the needles push pegs into a carrying plate. A rod (U) is put through the false warp, following the first pick, which is undone. The rod is pulled forward and held under the arm (j) shown in Plate 93. This pulls forward the needles corresponding to the lifts. The needles push small pegs into the carrying plate, which is then carried to the punching table to make the punched card. When punching is complete, the carrying plate is replaced in the mechanism, and the grid of needles (C) (Plate 93), is pushed down on to it, which replaces the pegs in the needlecase. The rod is removed, and the next pick is made in the same way.

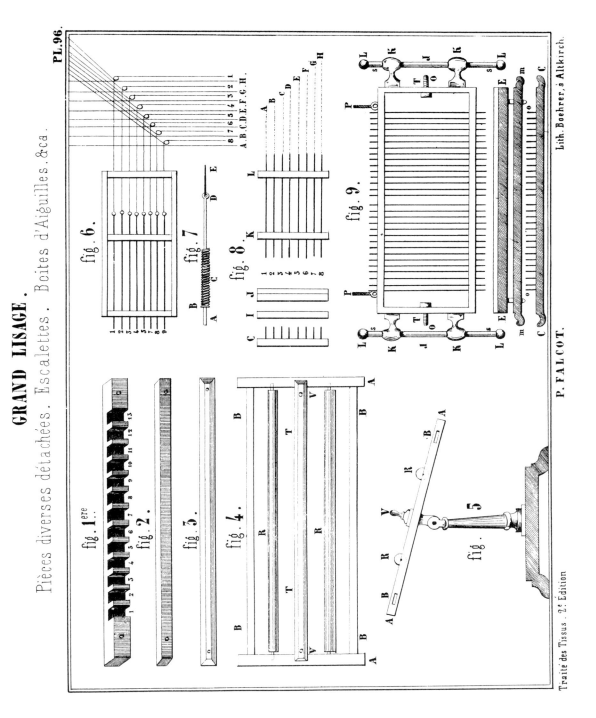

Plate 96 shows some of the parts of the apparatus illustrated in Plates 93–5. Figs. 1, 2 and 3 show the grooved board through which the bundles of threads pass at the back of the machine. Fig.4 shows the frame of rods which hold the paper draft while the replica is being woven. (Falcot's description ends here.)

Fig.9 shows the layout of the needlecase for the duplicating machine (Plate 102).

52

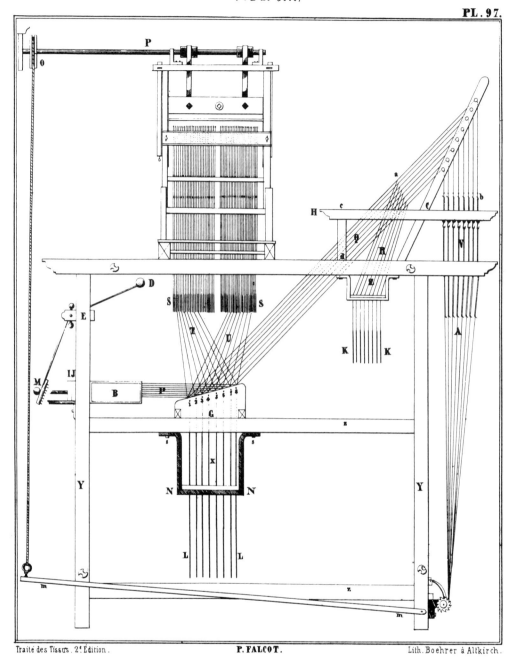

Traité des Tissus. 2ᵉ Édition .   **P. FALCOT.**   Lith. Boehrer à Altkirch.

Plates 97, 98, 99 and 100 show an improved high-speed machine for reading a design. The needlecase mechanism for the making of the pattern plates with pegs in a template is the same, the templates still have to be taken individually to the punching table for the cards to be punched. The rollers of the wheel reader are replaced by a bank of pulleys (Plate 98).

Plate 97 shows the three sets of cords in the system: those controlling the needles (P), those which take the pull of the design threads (Q), and those of the Jacquard mechanism; all three join in order over an oblique grill, and through a neck board (N) held in tension by weights (L).

LISAGE ACCÉLÉRÉ.

(Vu du coté de l'Accrochage.)

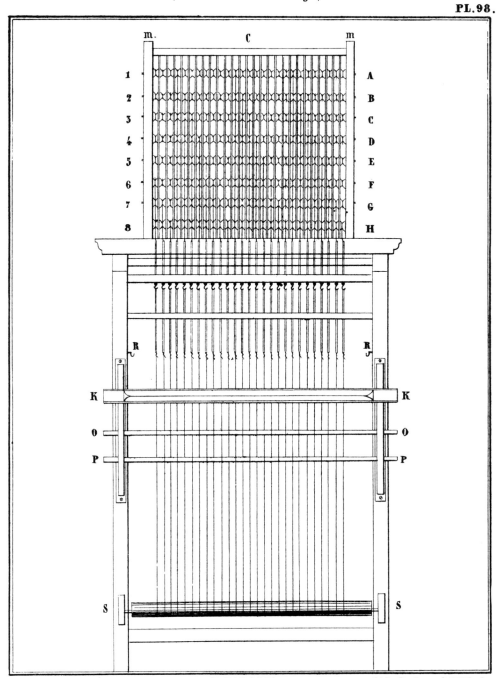

Traité des Tissus. 2ᵉ Édition.   P. FALCOT..   Lith. Boehrer à Altkirch.

Plate 98 shows the bank of pulleys – there is one for every thread. These take the place of the eight rollers in the drum reader (Plate 93). The whole of this mechanism is detachable, so a design can be made up on the threads in the same way as for the drum reader away from the mechanism, and then the frame can be hooked on for the making of the templates.

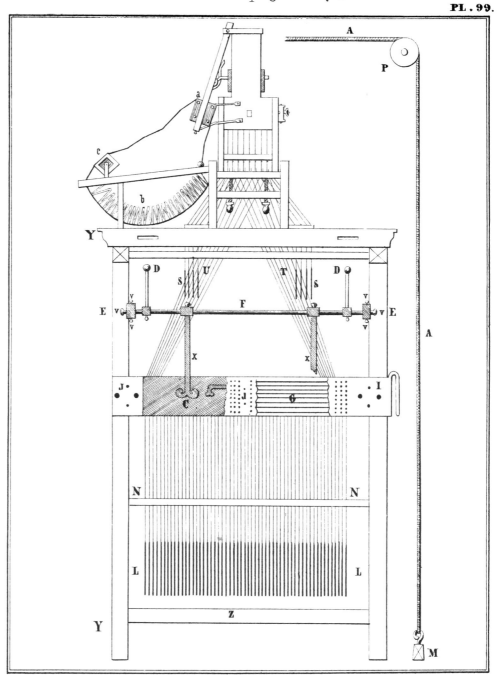

Traité des Tissus . 2ᵉ Edition.　　　　**P. FALCOT.**　　　　Luth. Boehrer à Altkirch.

Plate 99 shows a device for the repeat punching of cards. A card holder can be seen mounted at the top, driven over its cylinder by a pedal. This reads the design and motivates the Jacquard mechanism which pushes the pegs in the usual way into the pattern plate. It is easier, if making several copies of a design, to duplicate at the punching table rather than by running the cards through this system several times.

LISAGE ACCÉLÉRÉ.
Accrochage portatif.

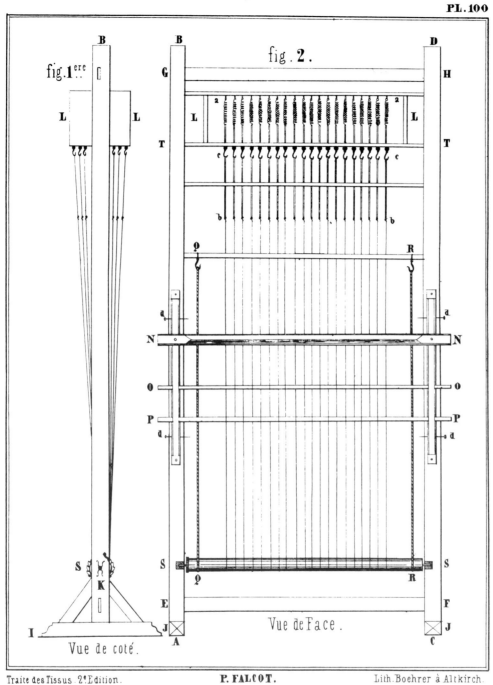

fig.1ere

fig. 2.

Vue de coté.

Vue de Face.

Traité des Tissus. 2ᵉ Edition.   P. FALCOT.   Lith. Boehrer à Altkirch.

Plate 100 shows the detachable coupling frame, with needles held on springs and passing through two retaining boards. All the procedures for putting in the cross, reading the draft etcetera are the same as described for the drum reader. This machine needs two people to work it, as the simple cannot be pulled through to the front for undoing; this has to be done at the back. The drum reader needs only one operator.

PRESSE
ou Machine à percer les cartons

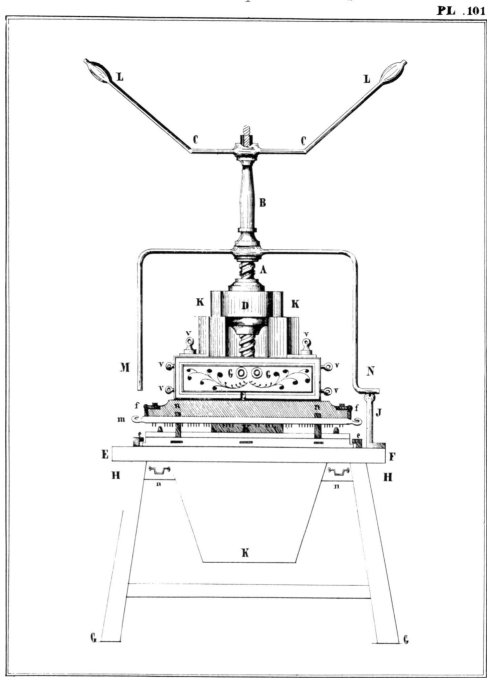

Traité des Tissus 2ᵉ Édition.   **P. FALCOT.**   Lith. Boehrer à Altkirch.

Plate 101 shows the punching table, a strong table with a heavy iron screw frame on top, turned by the bar M–N. The template, with its pegs, is taken out of the reader and placed at m. Under it, in a sliding case, is a card, held under a hinged plate which has holes conforming to the configuration of the loom. The screw is turned, and the plate descends on the matrix, forcing the pins on to the pegs held in the receiving board which punch the card (the waste falls into a trough under the table, K). The screw is unwound, and the card removed and replaced with a new one; the template is taken back to the reader and cleared, ready for the next card.

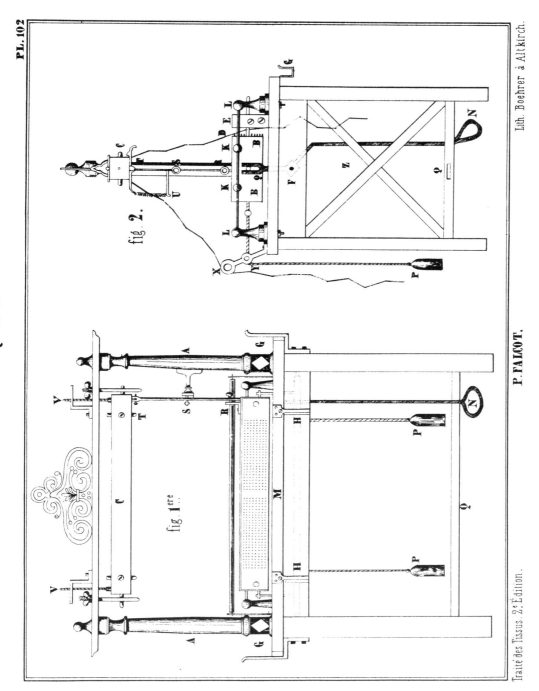

REPIQUAGE.

PL. 102

Lith. Boehrer à Altkirch.

P. FALCOT.

Traité des Tissus. 2.ᵉ Édition.

fig. 2.

fig. 1ᵉʳᵉ.

Plate 102 shows how cards can be reproduced without going through the process of reading again. The device carries a needlecase where the needles are backed with springs. The process is similar to the original marking by way of pegs pushed into a receiver to make a template which is then punched on the punching table. The cards are placed over the roller at the back and fed round the cylinder (C), with the first card held at the back of the needlecase. When the pedal (N) is pushed, the needlecase moves backwards; needles corresponding to holes in the card move the relevant pegs into the receiver. The operation is repeated card by card until the design has been completed.

LAÇAGE.
Table à couper les cartons.

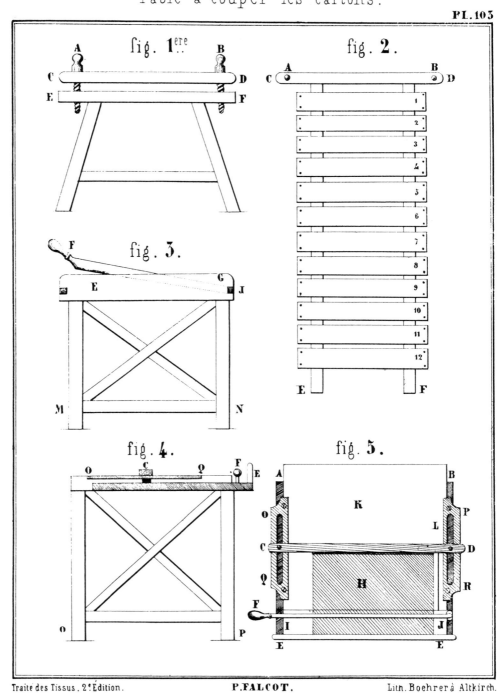

fig. 1ere

fig. 2.

fig. 3.

fig. 4.

fig. 5.

Traité des Tissus. 2ᵉ Édition.   P.FALCOT.   Litn.Boehrer à Altkirch.

Plate 103 Cards for the Jacquard were originally cut using a ruler and blade. However, a quicker and easier way was soon developed, as shown in figs. 3, 4 and 5. This is what we now call a guillotine (though Falcot, writing within living memory of the French Revolution, does not use the word). It is a sturdy table with a blade at the side and adjustable parameters for different sizes of card.

Plate 58 showed the method for lacing cards together. Here they are shown laid out on a trestle (fig.2); the press (fig.1) could be used to hold them if there are too many to fit on. Cards are numbered on the right; they may be organized in two sections if, for example, a brocade pattern is worked over a plain ground. The smaller cards are laced at the side, medium-sized ones in the middle as well, and the largest size has four lacings.

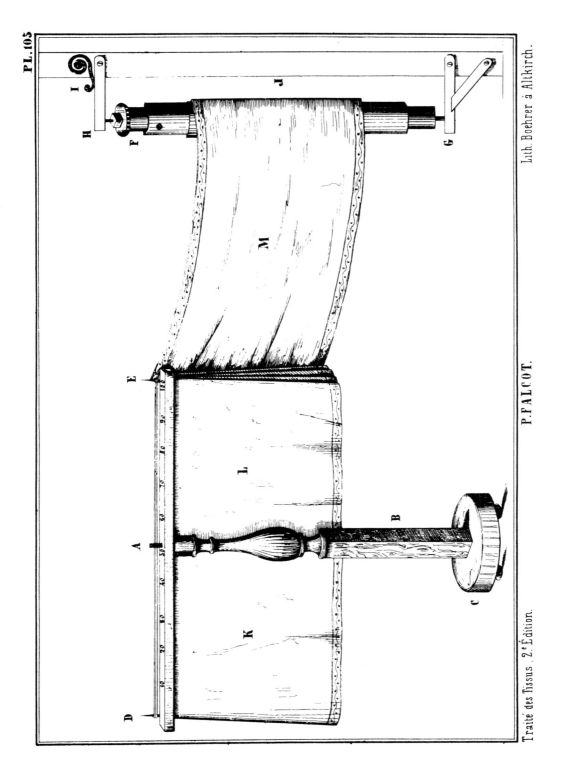

MÉTRAGE DES ÉTOFFES.

PL.105

Lith. Boehrer à Altkirch.

P.FALCOT.

Traité des Tissus . 2.ᵉ Édition.

Plate 105 A device for measuring cloth on a metre stick as it is taken off the front beam of the loom, shown held upright in a frame.

MOUVEMENT DE LÈVE ET BAISSE
Pour les lisses, au moyen de la mécanique Armure.

PL.109.

60

fig. 2.

fig. 1re

C
B————⊕————A
D
E
F————————F
G
H

C   A
D   B

Côté de { l'étui.   1 } Coté de la
                                                     2 } planchette

N ·· M. Planche à collets

4   2
3   · ·   1   1   2

N ▓▓▓▓▓▓▓▓▓▓▓ M
J ▓▓▓▓▓▓▓▓▓▓▓ I   } Croisement
m   m   alternatif
n   n   sur deux lisses.
P ——————————— O
L ——————————— K

H   E
F   G

Plate 109 shows the method by which shafts which both rise and fall can be incorporated in a Jacquard loom. There are various mechanisms which can operate this.
    There is no need to draft the background when shafts are used.

BATTANT À DOUBLES-BOITES.

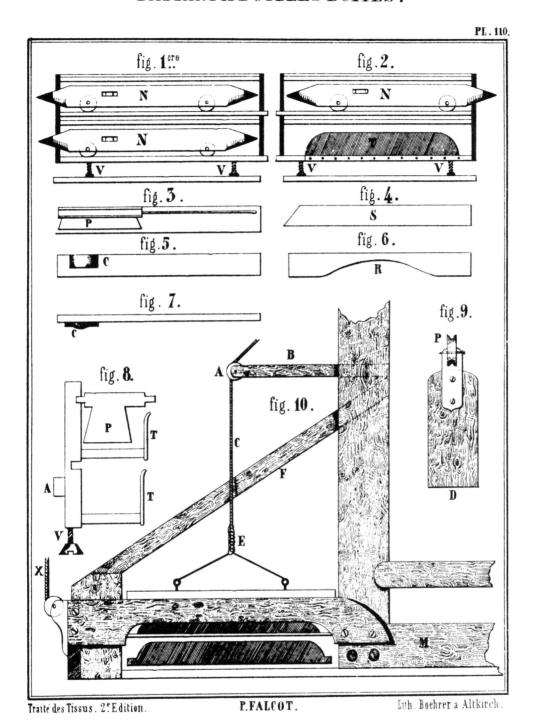

fig. 1.ᶜʳᵉ

fig. 2.

fig. 3.

fig. 4.

fig. 5.

fig. 6.

fig. 7.

fig. 8.

fig. 9.

fig. 10.

Traité des Tissus. 2ᶜ Edition.   P. FALCOT.   Lith. Boehrer a Altkirch.

Plate 110 shows the construction of a double-box batten. The mechanism of boxes, pickers and cords is the same as the simple box batten (see Plate 9); in addition, the boxes are movable, usually vertically. The boxes are connected to the hook mechanism of the Jacquard, and the punch card can incorporate controls for the hooks attached to the batten mechanism so the boxes rise or fall according to the design. A little-known advantage of the double-box batten is that it can be used with three shuttles if the sequences are carefully worked out; similarly a triple-box batten can operate with five shuttles.

LANCÉ.

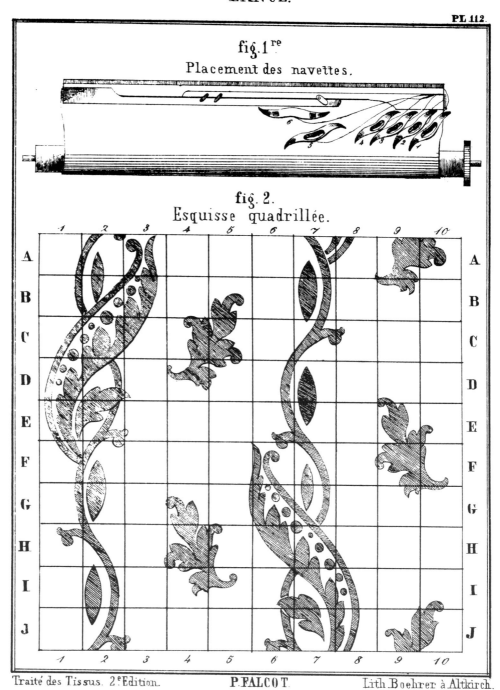

fig. 1re
Placement des navettes.

fig. 2.
Esquisse quadrillée.

Traité des Tissus. 2.ᵉ Edition. P. FALCOT. Lith. Boehrer à Altkirch.

Plate 112 shows a weft patterned fabric where the design may require several colours in different sheds to make one pick. There will often be long floats left on the back of the fabric which need to be cut afterwards.

When dealing with a number of shuttles on a wide cloth, the weaver had an assistant (usually a child) to keep the shuttles in their correct order. The shuttles are placed at the side in their order of arrival, which helps keep the threads untangled and the selvedge neat. Where some shuttles are used only intermittently, they should be kept away from the selvedge, as 5 and 6 are in fig.1

BROCHÉS.

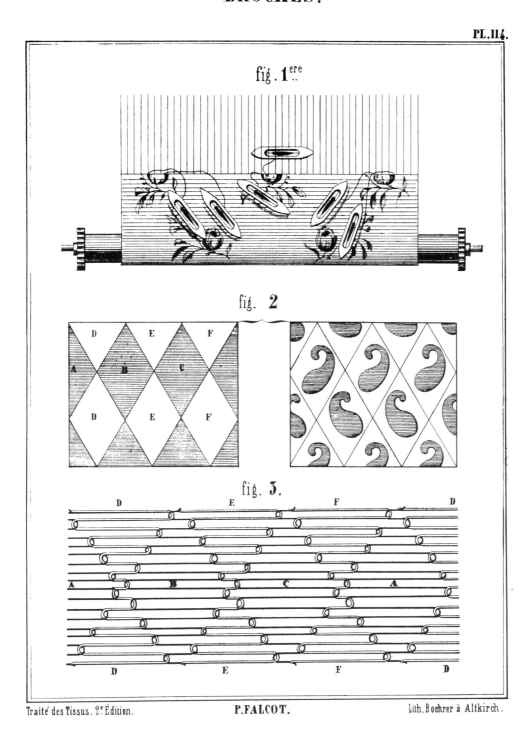

fig. 1ere

fig. 2

fig. 3.

Traité des Tissus. 2ᵉ Édition.   **P.FALCOT.**   Lith.Boehrer à Altkirch.

Plate 114 shows a method of brocade patterning which allows for the use of precious threads, such as gold and silver, as no long floats are involved. As shown in fig.1, the motifs are made separately, using small shuttles which remain in place. Different colours can be used across the warp, each group having its own colouring. When densely packed, the fabric is bulky, and padding is needed on the front beam to avoid flattening the motifs and distorting the fabric. This fabric is always woven with the right side down, and the design can be used in conjunction with other weft patterning.

Linked brocade, as shown in fig.3 is the richest and most solid, but time-consuming.

PRESSES DIVERSES
pour chiner.

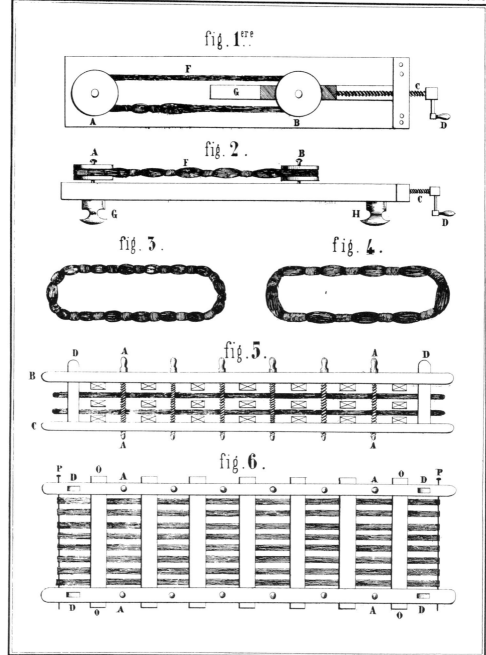

fig.1ᵉʳᵉ

fig.2.

fig.3.

fig.4.

fig.5.

fig.6.

Traité des Tissus. 2ᵉ Édition.   **P.FALCOT.**   Lith. Boehrer à Altkirch.

Plate 117 shows the method of making what we should today call ikat, though the term *chiné* includes painted as well as dyed warps.

The threads can be dyed in the hank, tied in various spacings as shown in figs. 3 and 4; or held in a press for the dyeing of several hanks together (figs. 5 and 6), though this latter makes overdyeing difficult. Figs. 1 and 2 show a method of holding a hank in tension for tying – the adjustable pulley (B) allows for a variety of hank size to be dyed. For regular *chiné*, the warp is first made in small sections, and then tied for dyeing. A whole warp can be made and put on the loom, woven at the ends and at intervals to hold it in place, and then taken off and dyed.

CHINÉS

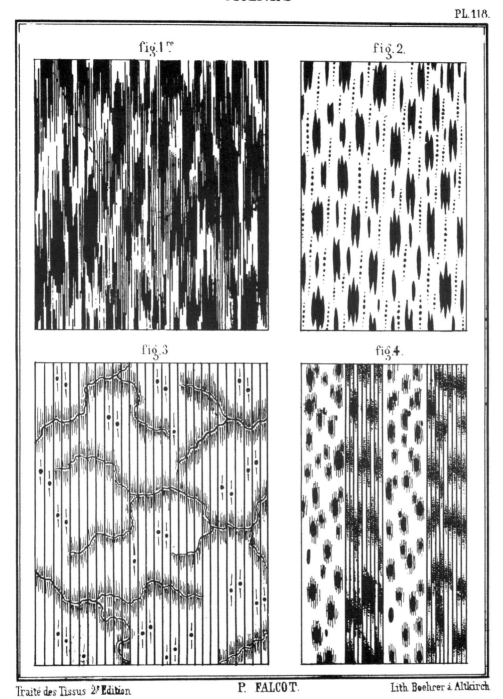

fig. 1re

fig. 2.

fig. 3

fig. 4.

Traité des Tissus 2ᵉ Édition   P. FALCOT.   Lith Boehrer à Altkirch

Plate 118 shows four examples of *chiné* designs. Fig.1 is a simple random effect, while the others are more controlled. The bands in which the warp has been tied can be seen clearly.

The term should not be confused with *crêpe-de-chine*, which has no relation to it, being a very elastic fabric constructed with alternating picks of S and Z highly twisted threads.

ESQUISSES
pour ombrés et fondus.

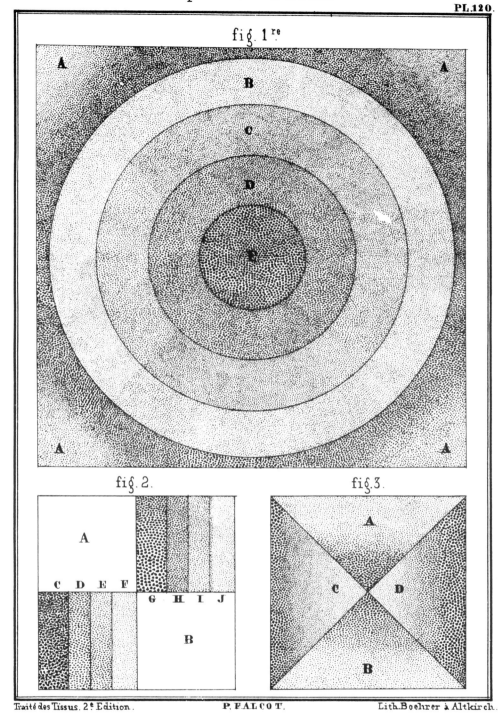

fig. 1re.

fig. 2.

fig. 3.

Traité des Tissus. 2e Edition.   P. FALCOT.   Lith.Boehrer à Altkirch.

Plates 120 and 121 show woven shading effects. These were unheard-of fifty years before Falcot wrote. However, through what he calls 'the genius of invention', the most delicate graduations of shading can be achieved.

'Threads need to be very fine, preferably silk; and colours of warp and weft are usually of similar shades, but they can be contrasting. To avoid sharp changes, a high warp count is needed. It is a complicated process, needing great knowledge of weaving.'

If one imagines a central point from which the surrounding colours shade out, the interlacing in the weave design is arranged so that the weft floats become gradually shorter towards the centre of the design, and the effect of the warp takes over. **Plate 121** shows drafts of this effect, and **Plate 120** their possible use in a fabric.

FONDUS.

mises en carte.

fig:1.ere

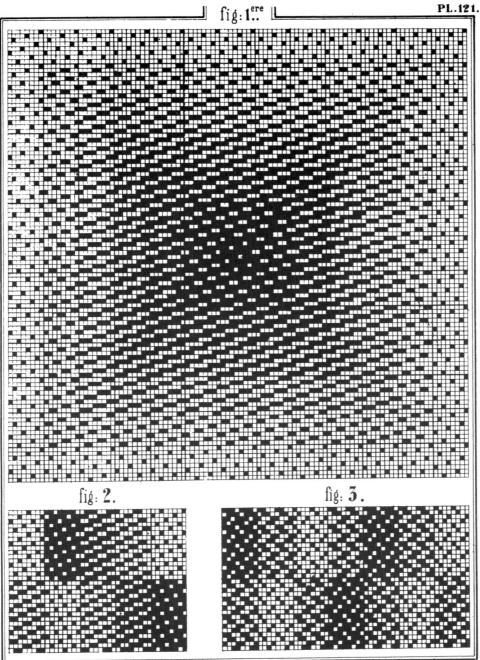

fig: 2.

fig: 3.

Traité des Tissus. 2.ᵉÉdition.   P.FALCOT.   Lith.G.Eckardt,Mulhouse

DAMASSÉS.

Mouvement des lisses par effet de lève et baisse.

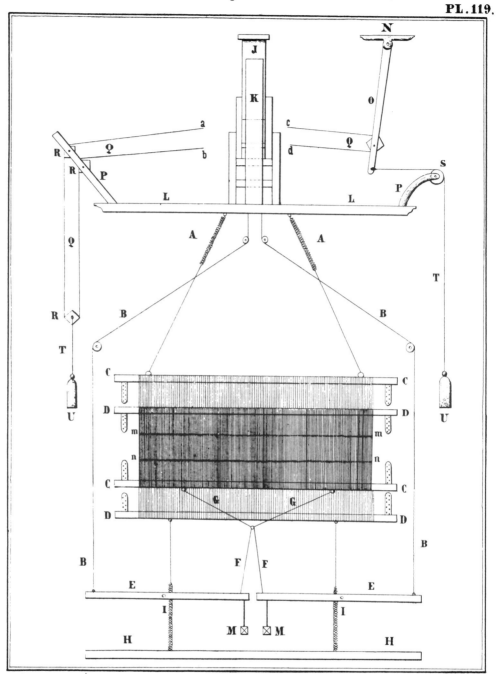

Traité des Tissus. 2ᵉ Édition.   **P. FALCOT.**   Lith. Boehrer à Altkirch.

Plate 119 concerns damasks – self-patterned fabrics made with the patterning contained in a single warp.

When weaving with a Jacquard, the scope of the loom can be extended by using shafts as well as the harness. This is done by putting several threads (up to a maximum of eight) through the eyelets of a single mail. These are then placed through shafts where one rises and the other remains at rest; thus for every movement of the mail, there will be an interlacing of the several warp threads which it contains. By this means, a design which, say, over 400 hooks could weave 10cm, could be extended to 20cm by putting two threads to a hook, or 30cm with three, and so on.

Sometimes damask is woven with one thread to a mail, interspersed with one thread going through the shaft – the former makes the pattern, the latter the background.

RÉGULATEUR-COMPENSATEUR

des charges ou contre-poids pour les métiers à Lisses ou lames.

PL.123.

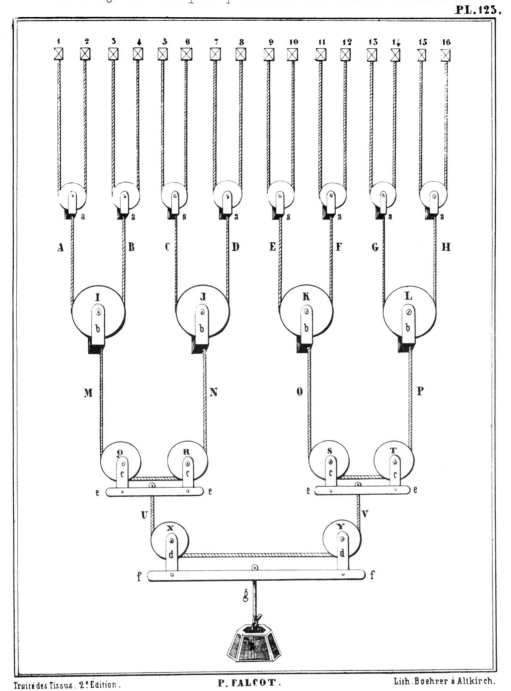

Traité des Tissus. 2.ᵉ Édition.

P. FALCOT.

Lith. Boehrer à Altkirch.

Plate 123 shows a compensating weighting system for shaft looms.

ÉTOFFES À DOUBLE FACE.

en étoffes doubles.

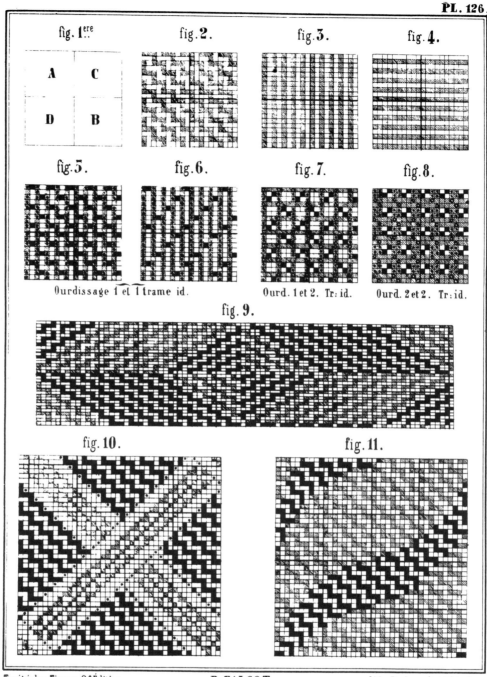

fig. 1ère.

fig. 2.

fig. 3.

fig. 4.

fig. 5.

fig. 6.

fig. 7.

fig. 8.

Ourdissage 1 et 1 trame id.

Ourd. 1 et 2. Tr: id.

Ourd. 2 et 2. Tr: id.

fig. 9.

fig. 10.

fig. 11.

Traité des Tissus. 2.ᵉ Édition.   **P. FALCOT.**   Lith. Boehrer à Altkirch.

Plate 126 demonstrates the principle of drafting for double-cloth, for a square divided in four. Fig.2 shows how the draft would be shaded in for a plain weave, with the grey squares being those for drafting the top cloth; the bottom cloth to be drafted in black and white as usual.

For weaves other than plain weave, the colouring is made for every alternative warp or weft thread (figs. 3 and 4); each cloth is therefore drafted on the thread to which it relates (figs. 5 and 6).

ÉTOFFES DOUBLES
Armures diverses.

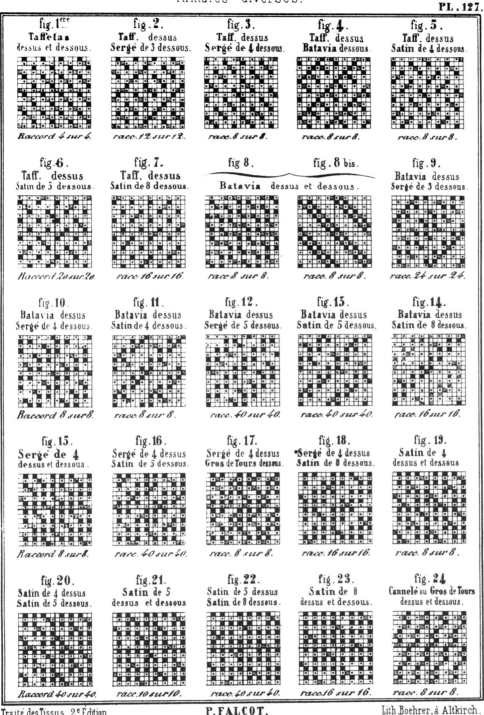

fig.1ère
Taffetas
dessus et dessous.
Raccord 4 sur 4.

fig.2.
Taff. dessus
Serge de 3 dessous.
race.12 sur 12.

fig.3.
Taff. dessus
Serge de 4 dessous.
race.8 sur 8.

fig.4.
Taff. dessus
Batavia dessous.
race.8 sur 8.

fig.5.
Taff. dessus
Satin de 4 dessous.
race.8 sur 8.

fig.6.
Taff. dessus
Satin de 5 dessous.
Raccord 20 sur 20.

fig.7.
Taff. dessus
Satin de 8 dessous.
race.16 sur 16.

fig 8.   fig.8 bis.
Batavia dessus et dessous.
race.8 sur 8.   *race.8 sur 8.*

fig.9.
Batavia dessus
Serge de 3 dessous.
race.24 sur 24.

fig.10.
Batavia dessus
Serge de 4 dessous.
Raccord 8 sur 8.

fig.11.
Batavia dessus
Satin de 4 dessous.
race.8 sur 8.

fig.12.
Batavia dessus
Serge de 5 dessous.
race.40 sur 40.

fig.13.
Batavia dessus
Satin de 5 dessous.
race.40 sur 40.

fig.14.
Batavia dessus
Satin de 8 dessous.
race.16 sur 16.

fig.15.
Serge de 4
dessus et dessous.
Raccord 8 sur 8.

fig.16.
Serge de 4 dessus
Satin de 5 dessous.
race.40 sur 40.

fig.17.
Serge de 4 dessus
Gros de Tours dessous.
race.8 sur 8.

fig.18.
•Serge de 4 dessus
Satin de 8 dessous.
race.16 sur 16.

fig.19.
Satin de 4
dessus et dessous
race.8 sur 8.

fig.20.
Satin de 4 dessus
Satin de 5 dessous.
Raccord 40 sur 40.

fig.21.
Satin de 5
dessus et dessous
race.10 sur 10.

fig.22.
Satin de 5 dessus
Satin de 8 dessous.
race.40 sur 40.

fig.23.
Satin de 8
dessus et dessous.
race.16 sur 16.

fig.24
Cannelé ou Gros de Tours
dessus et dessous.
race.8 sur 8.

Traité des Tissus. 2e Édition.   **P.FALCOT.**   Lith.Boehrer, à Altkirch.

Plate 127 A selection of drafts for double-cloths.

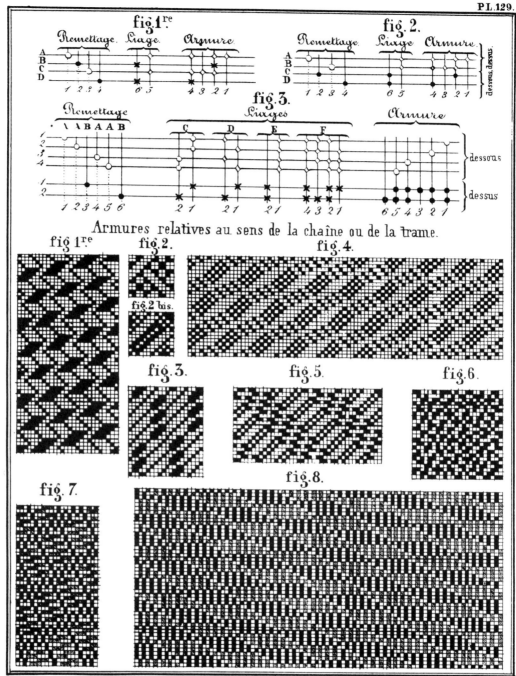

Armures relatives au sens de la chaîne ou de la trame.

Plate 129 shows the basic principles for the construction of matelassé, a padded fabric which can be made in a large combination of yarns and weaves. The cloth is a basic double-weave enclosing a thicker padding thread in either warp or weft – the former makes a better quality cloth but is more difficult to make because of the wear on the padding cords in the reed. The tying of the two cloths together is done with a fine additional warp on a separate beam; in some cases, e.g. when the fabric design is in lozenges, this can be in a contrasting colour, and makes an attractive regular spot. Several methods of organizing the tying threads are shown (fig.3 C, D, E warp ties, F weft tie).

DÉCOCHEMENTS RECTILIGNES.

(Principes.)

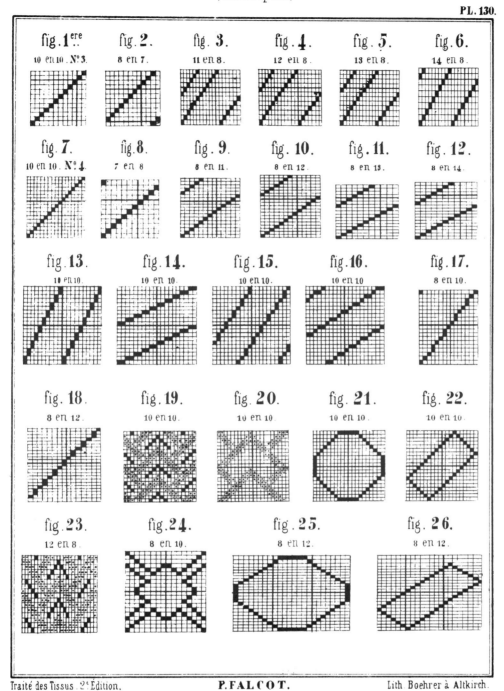

fig. 1ere. — 10 en 10. N° 3.
fig. 2. — 8 en 7.
fig. 3. — 11 en 8.
fig. 4. — 12 en 8.
fig. 5. — 13 en 8.
fig. 6. — 14 en 8.

fig. 7. — 10 en 10. N° 4.
fig. 8. — 7 en 8.
fig. 9. — 8 en 11.
fig. 10. — 8 en 12.
fig. 11. — 8 en 13.
fig. 12. — 8 en 14.

fig. 13. — 10 en 10.
fig. 14. — 10 en 10.
fig. 15. — 10 en 10.
fig. 16. — 10 en 10.
fig. 17. — 8 en 10.

fig. 18. — 8 en 12.
fig. 19. — 10 en 10.
fig. 20. — 10 en 10.
fig. 21. — 10 en 10.
fig. 22. — 10 en 10.

fig. 23. — 12 en 8.
fig. 24. — 8 en 10.
fig. 25. — 8 en 12.
fig. 26. — 8 en 12.

Traité des Tissus. 2ᵉ Édition. **P. FALCOT.** Lith. Boehrer à Altkirch.

Plate 130 shows drafts for grading angled lines. On symmetrical paper (fig.1) a diagonal line at 45 degrees can be made using sequential threads. This line moves to the vertical as the fabric (and therefore the draft paper) has a higher proportion of warp (figs. 2 to 6) or to the horizontal if there is more weft (figs. 8 to 12).

DÉCOCHEMENTS CURVILIGNES.
(Principes.)

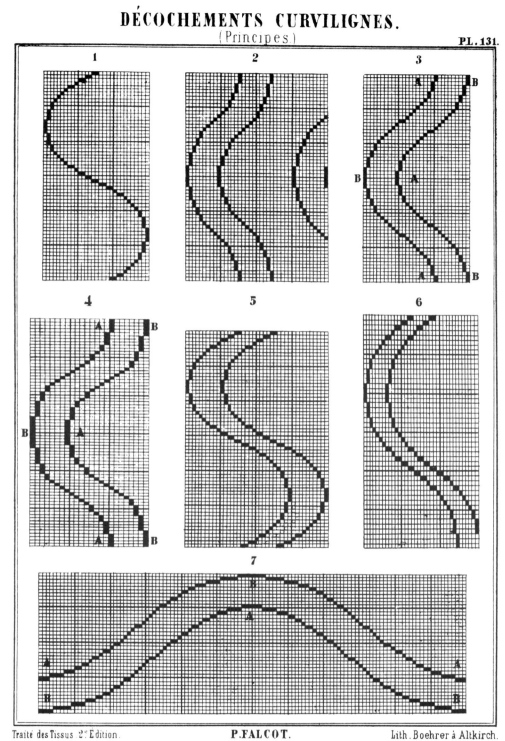

Traité des Tissus 2.ᵉ Édition.   **P.FALCOT.**   Lith.Boehrer à Altkirch.

Plate 131 shows the drafting for curved motifs, which can be either regular or irregular. Note that the angles of double curves may not always be the same – in fig.3, the curves at A and B differ.

In figs. 5 and 6 it can be seen that the juxtaposition of two identical drafts produces a narrowing in the appearance of the curves.

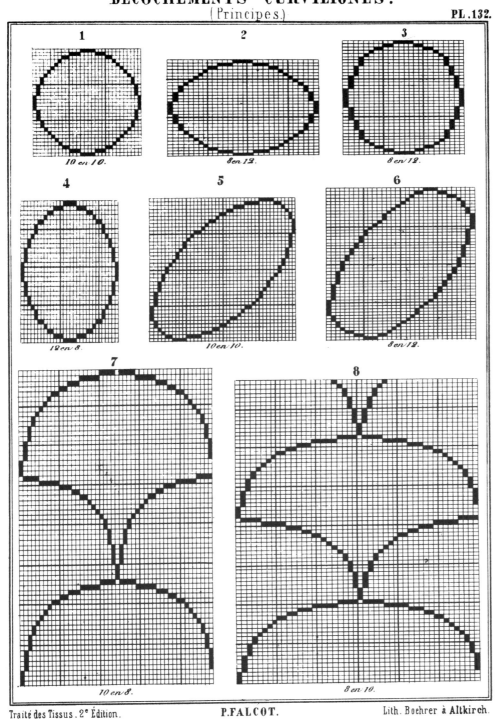

Traité des Tissus. 2ᵉ Édition.   P.FALCOT.   Lith. Boehrer à Altkirch.

Plate 132 demonstrates that although the transposition of rectangular designs on to different scale paper will still give a recognizable variant of the pattern (Plate 130), a very different shape results when curved designs are transposed. Compare the circle on 10 × 10 (fig.1) with the same draft on 8 × 12 (fig.2), and it will be seen that the draft has to be modified to obtain the shape required, as in fig.3.

76

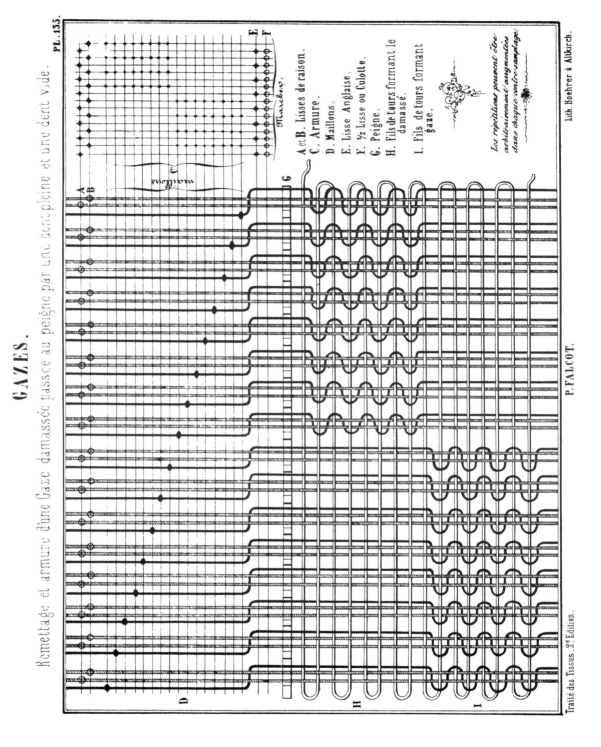

Lith. Boehrer à Altkirch.

P. FALCOT.

Traité des Tissus. 2e Édition.

Plates 135, 136 and 137 concern gauze, which in the nineteenth century was a very common fabric. A light, plain weave cloth, woven with one thread to a dent in the reed would be unstable, but an invention which Falcot calls 'one of the most ingenious in all weaving' allows for a more stable cloth to be constructed, by means of the controlled turning of one warp thread around its neighbour.

Plate 135 shows a draft and a diagram of a fabric alternating areas of gauze weave with a plain weave background, the special turning thread (shown black) working sometimes in its special role, and sometimes weaving in an ordinary fashion, working with the left-hand shaft of the pair at the back.

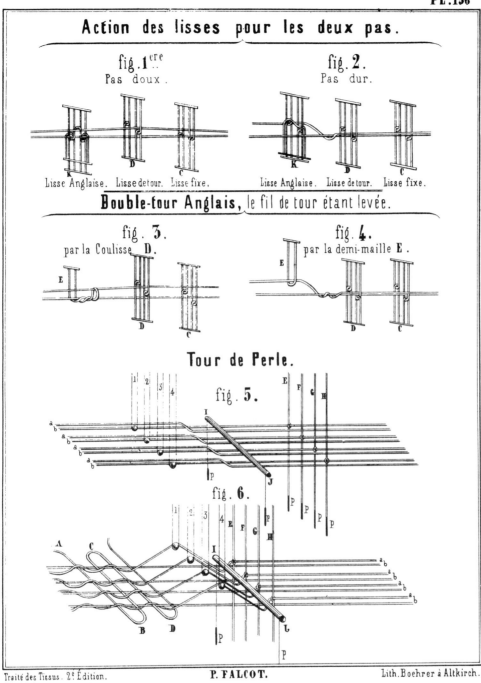

Action des lisses pour les deux pas.

fig.1ere.
Pas doux.

Lisse Anglaise. Lisse de tour. Lisse fixe.

fig.2.
Pas dur.

Lisse Anglaise. Lisse de tour. Lisse fixe.

Bouble-tour Anglais, le fil de tour étant levée.

fig.3.
par la Coulisse D.

fig.4.
par la demi-maille E.

Tour de Perle.

fig.5.

fig.6.

Plate 136 shows the configuration of warp threads and shafts, with the half heddle (doup) by which the turning thread is controlled to move over the fixed thread. The half heddles in fig.5 have small beads at the bottom through which the turning thread also passes, which allows them to make a one-and-a-half turn around the fixed thread.

GAZES.

Mouvements divers des fils de tours, simples et doubles.

78

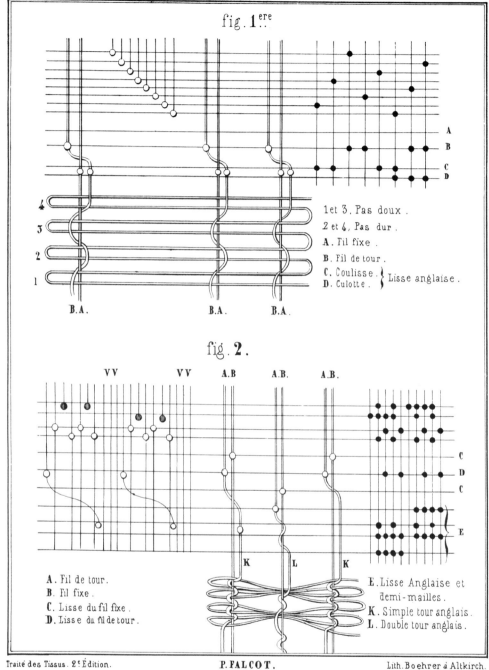

fig. 1.ᵉʳᵉ

A
B
C
D

1 et 3 . Pas doux .

2 et 4 , Pas dur .

A . Fil fixe .

B . Fil de tour .

C . Coulisse . } Lisse anglaise .
D . Culotte .

4
3
2
1

B.A.   B.A.   B.A.

fig. 2.

V V   V V   A.B.   A.B.   A.B.

C
D
C

E

A . Fil de tour.
B . Fil fixe .
C . Lisse du fil fixe .
D . Lisse du fil de tour .

K   L   K

E . Lisse Anglaise et
demi-mailles .

K . Simple tour anglais .
L . Double tour anglais .

Traité des Tissus . 2ᵉ Édition.   **P. FALCOT.**   Lith. Boehrer à Altkirch.

Plate 137 shows configurations for various different gauzes.

METIERS MECANIQUES UNIS A LA BARRE.

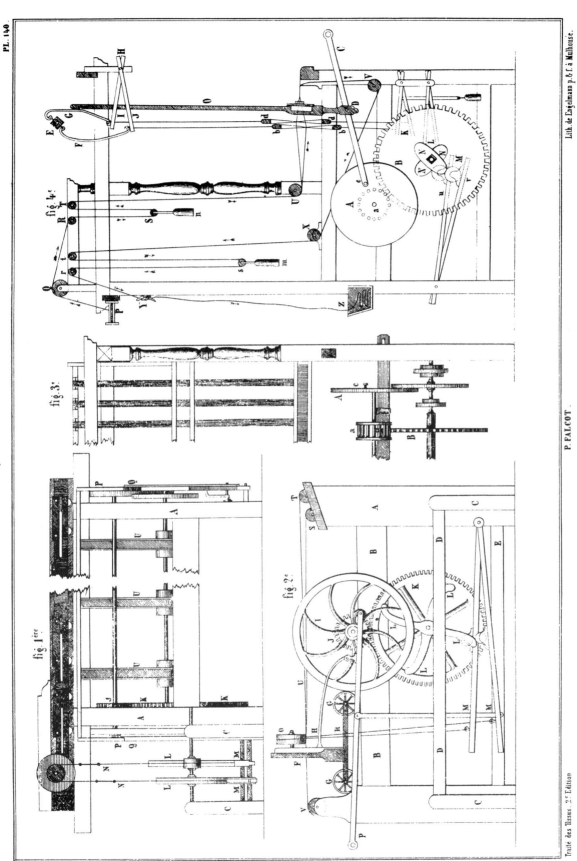

fig. 1ère

fig. 2e

fig. 3.

fig. 4e

Traité des Tissus. 2e Édition

P. FALCOT.

Lith de Engelmann p. & f. à Mulhouse.

Plate 140 shows a loom developed for the weaving of ribbons, a necessity because their narrowness and cheapness required a loom which could combine speed and the ability to make several pieces at once. This loom could make twenty-four to thirty pieces at once, but the quality was not as good as with the handloom shown in Plate 141.

RUBANS.
Métier à basse-lisse.

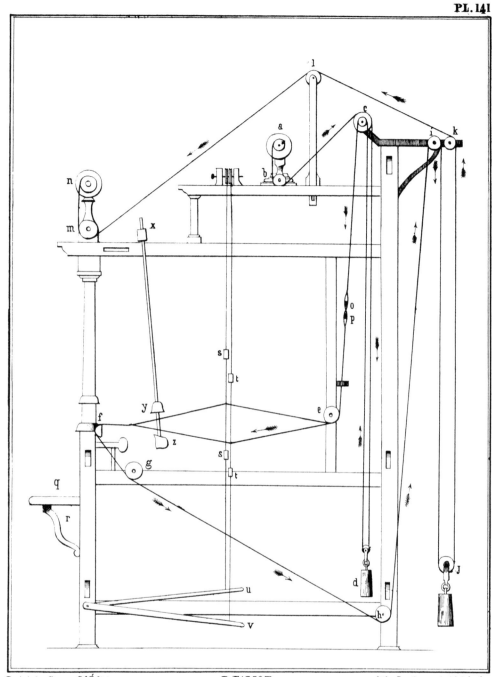

Traité des Tissus. 2⁵ Édition .   **P. FALCOT.**   Lith. Boehrer à Altkirch .

Plate 141 Falcot describes ribbons in his time as important, indispensable and ephemeral. The difficulty of making them led to specialization, with Lyons for once having to concede its weaving superiority to St Etienne. Whereas design faults in cloth can be hidden in folds and seams, ribbons display every detail of the cloth, front, back and sides, and so need to be planned and woven with great care.

The loom shown here (sometimes called a swivel loom) is one which can be used for most plain ribbons – it is elegantly designed to need little depth. The back beam is at a, and the direction of the warp is shown by the arrows to the breast beam at f, the woven ribbon then follows back over the loom to roll on to the beam at n. An additional reed is placed between the back cross (o–p) and the roller (e) to help separate the threads.

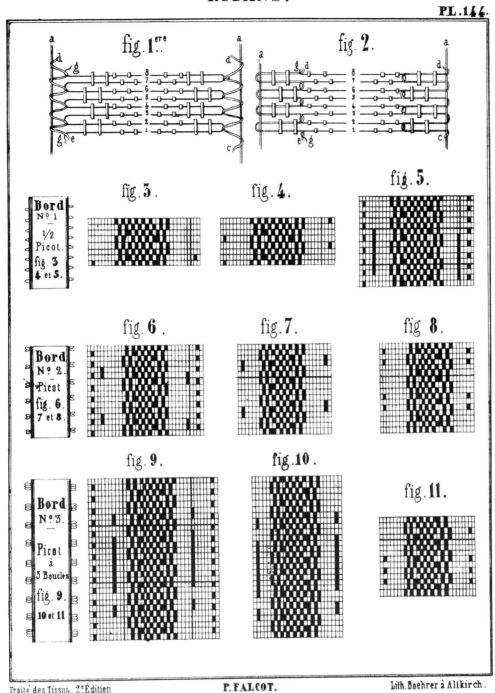

Traité des Tissus. 2.ᵉ Édition.

P. FALCOT.

Lith. Boehrer à Altkirch.

Plate 144 shows two ways of finishing ribbon edges. These are important as, unlike fabric selvedges, they are always visible.

Figs. 1 and 2 show a border made with an extra shuttle weaving at each side, catching on one side into the main structure, and on the other over an additional warp thread passing through the reed a few dents away from the edge of the ribbon.

The rest of the plate shows weft-effect borders where one or more threads of metal or horsehair pass through the reed away from the main warp, and form a base for the shuttle to catch as it passes over. Various configurations are shown; for example, border 1 (fig.3) is called half-picot. It can be of different intervals, either eight picks long with an interval of six between the points, or four picks long, when it is called rat-tooth.

PAPIERS DIVERS

pour la mise en carte.

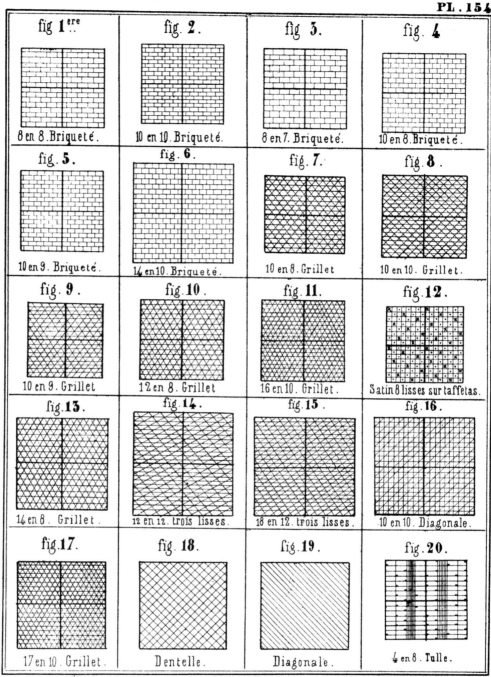

fig 1ere — 8 en 8. Briqueté.
fig. 2. — 10 en 10. Briqueté.
fig. 3. — 8 en 7. Briqueté.
fig. 4 — 10 en 8. Briqueté.
fig. 5. — 10 en 9. Briqueté.
fig. 6. — 14 en 10. Briqueté.
fig. 7. — 10 en 8. Grillet
fig. 8. — 10 en 10. Grillet.
fig. 9. — 10 en 9. Grillet
fig. 10. — 12 en 8. Grillet.
fig. 11. — 16 en 10. Grillet.
fig. 12. — Satin 8 lisses sur taffetas.
fig. 13. — 14 en 8. Grillet.
fig. 14. — 12 en 12. trois lisses.
fig. 15. — 18 en 12. trois lisses.
fig. 16. — 10 en 10. Diagonale.
fig. 17. — 17 en 10. Grillet.
fig. 18. — Dentelle.
fig. 19. — Diagonale.
fig. 20. — 4 en 8. Tulle.

Traité des Tissus. 2? Édition. **P. FALCOT.** Lith. Boehrer à Altkirch.

Plate 154 shows various papers for drafting shawls. The paper called (for obvious reasons) briquette allows for a quarter of the design to be drafted easily, as each briquette represents two cords of the Jacquard harness; and each cord holds an eyelet with two warp threads in it.

The Grillet paper, named after its inventor, aims to display the design in three directions, but proved too difficult to read and was abandoned.

Dimensions for these papers vary, just as for the draft papers shown in Plate 40.

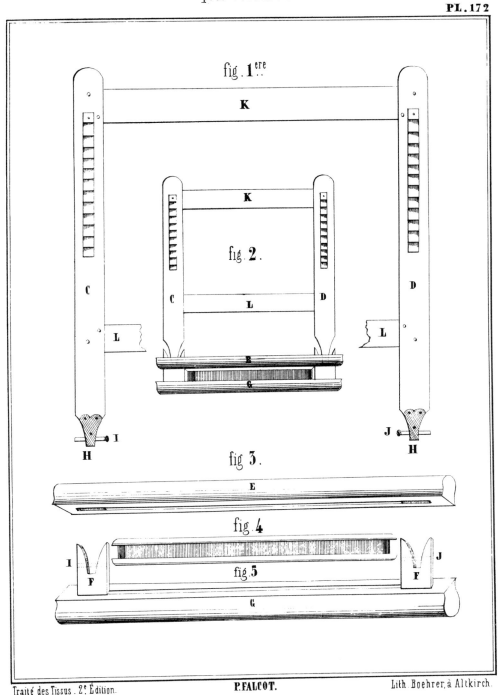

fig. 1ᵉʳᵉ

K

fig. 2.

K

C

L

D

C

D

L

L

B

G

I

H

J

H

fig 3.

E

fig. 4

I

F

J

F

fig. 5

G

Traité des Tissus. 2ᵉ Édition.   P. FALCOT.   Lith. Boehrer, à Altkirch.

Plate 172 shows a batten specially designed for use when weaving velvet. Velvet is woven using grooved metal rods which are inserted in the shed over which some warp ends are looped. With a conventional batten the weft would not beat back against the rod as its depth would hold the shed open; so a special batten is used where the base can swing forwards so that the pick is pushed up against the rod at an oblique angle – the weighted bottom part of the batten swings on the pins (I and J).

VELOURS.

Ustensiles.   Coupe du Velours-Soie.

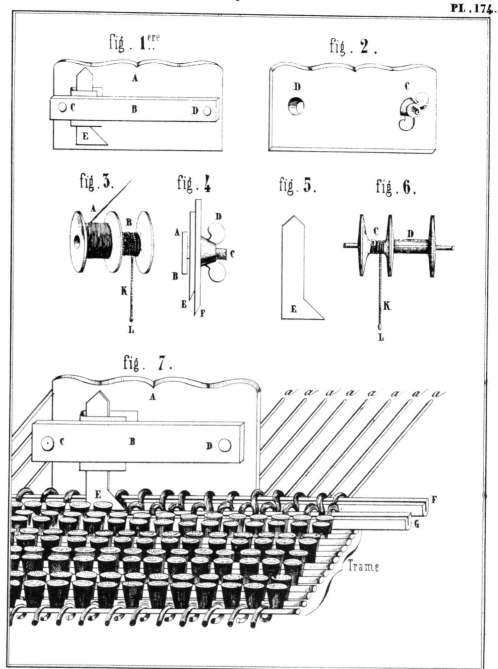

fig. 1ère.

fig. 2.

fig. 3.   fig. 4.   fig. 5.   fig. 6.

fig. 7.

Traité des Tissus. 2.ᵉ Édition.   **P. FALCOT.**   Lith. Roehrer à Altkirch.

Plate 174 shows (fig.7) the rods F and G in place with the front one being cut. Figs. 1 and 2 show the cutter in detail; the depth of the blade is adjustable by means of the screws as shown in fig.4. The cutter slides across the fabric, the blade fitting as shown into the groove in the rod.

Figs. 3 and 6 show the bobbins used when figured velvet is made on a Jacquard loom; the warp threads are held individually in a creel, rather than on a beam, counterweighted by a weighted thread B–K–L.

USTENSILES POUR VELOURS.

Sinuosités du poil, vu au microscope.

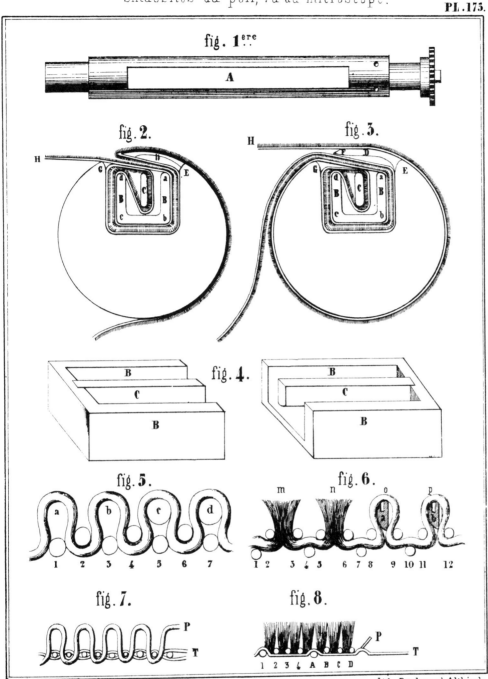

fig. 1ere

A

fig. 2.

fig. 3.

fig. 4.

fig. 5.

fig. 6.

fig. 7.

fig. 8.

Traité des Tissus. 2ᵉ Édition.   P. FALCOT.   Lith. Boehrer à Altkirch.

Plate 175 shows the special arrangement of the front beam for velvet. This avoids damage to the pile which would occur if the fabric was wound on in the usual way. Fig.1 shows the beam hollowed out; this holds a box (fig.4). Figs. 2 and 3 show the arrangement of the box in the beam with the velvet passing through; the fabric is held in tension on the wrong side by the angles in the box; the pile side only passes over the beam C which is itself covered with velvet. The fabric passes off the beam and is folded gently into a box under the loom.

Figs. 5 to 8 show the structure of the velvet in close-up. Fig.5 shows curled, uncut velvet; two rods can be seen still in place, the others have been removed, leaving loops, separated by one pick. Fig.6 shows cut velvet, with two rods also in place. Figs. 7 and 8 show velvet with an interwoven pile; 7 is in plain weave and 8 is twill.

The cutting of velvet by using a blade at the end of each rod developed with the use of cotton to give a cheaper velvet.

TAPIS.

Manière d'obtenir le velouté.

Formation du Noeud.   Effet du Tranchefil.

Traité des Tissus. 2ᵉ Édition.   **P. FALCOT.**   Lith. Boehrer à Altkirch.

Plate 178 Pile weaving on a high-warp loom. The two diagrams show the method for making a pile by means of a filler rod over which the weft is knotted; after that it is held in place by a pick of hemp woven in plain weave. The rod is removed to leave loops (see Plate 181). The cartoon can be seen at the top of the warp.

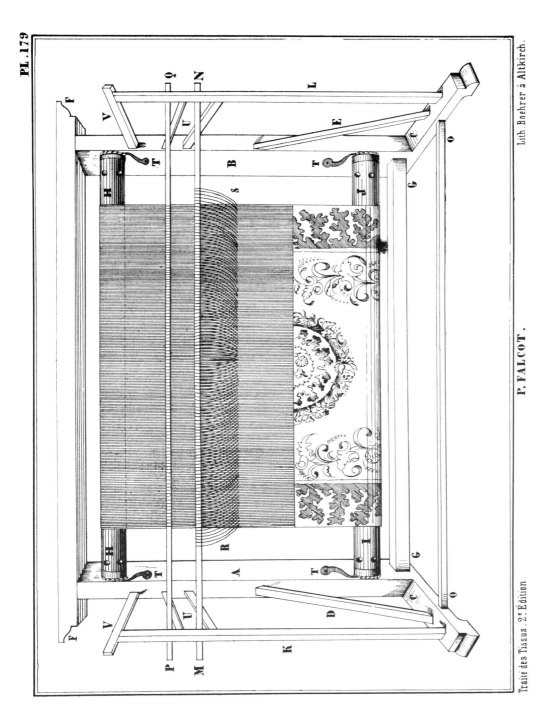

Lith. Boehrer à Altkirch.

P. FALCOT.

Traité des Tissus. 2ᵉ Édition.

Plate 179 shows a high-warp tapestry loom. They can be as large as 5m high and 15m wide, but whatever their size they are made on the same principle, as shown here. The warp threads are paired into odd and even threads by means of the stick P–Q.

The beams at the top and bottom are held by fixed tension, as the warp needs to be firmly maintained. Heddles R and S allow the back pairs of threads to be pulled forwards for weaving; the front ones can be easily picked out by hand.

The loom would be arranged so that the weavers would have the light from behind and a little to one side of them. Several weavers would work at one time on a tapestry.

MÉTIER VERTICAL POUR TAPIS.

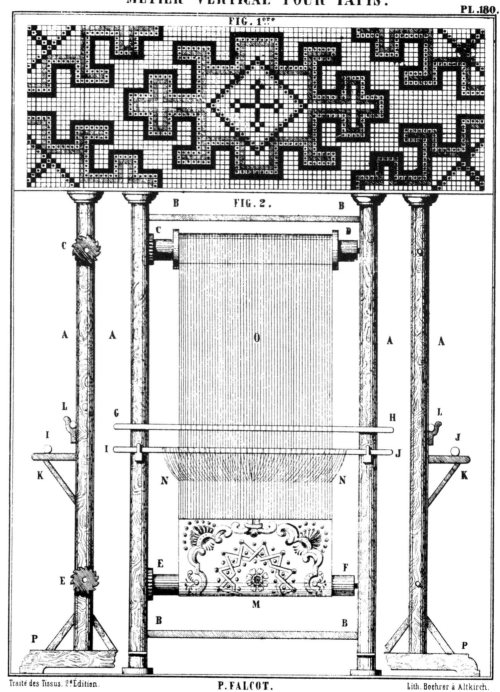

FIG. 1ère

FIG. 2.

Traité des Tissus. 2ᵉ Édition.

P. FALCOT.

Lith. Boehrer à Altkirch.

Plate 180 Alternative design of vertical tapestry or rug loom.

TAPIS.

Ourdissage et ustensiles divers.

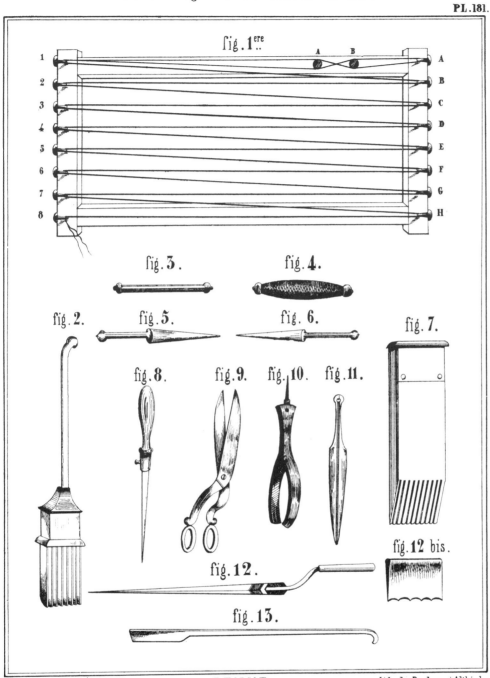

fig.1ᵉʳᵉ.

fig.3. fig.4.

fig.2. fig.5. fig.6. fig.7.

fig.8. fig.9. fig.10. fig.11.

fig.12 bis.

fig.12.

fig.13.

Traité des Tissus. 2ᵉ Édition.   P. FALCOT.   Lith. de Boehrer à Altkirch.

Plate 181 shows some of the tools which every tapestry weaver would have had in his personal toolkit. These include an ivory comb or beater (figs. 2 and 7); bobbins or flutes (figs. 3, 4, 5 and 6) which replace the shuttle and bobbin used in ordinary weaving; a punch (fig.8); scissors with curved handles for cutting pile knots (fig.9); pincers (fig.10); a pin (fig.11); a scraper (fig.12); and the filler rod (fig.13) in varying sizes to give different depths of pile.

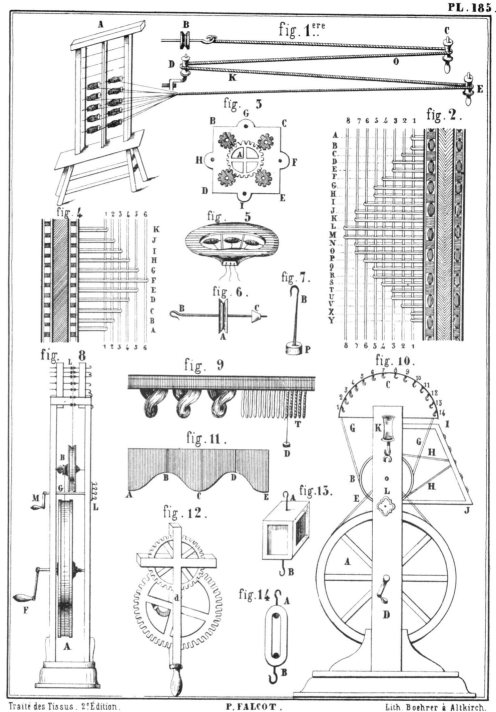

Traité des Tissus . 2ᵉ Édition .　　　　P. FALCOT .　　　　Lith. Boehrer à Altkirch.

Plate 185 shows the various tools used in the manufacture of *passementerie*, which involves a huge variety of twistings and counter-twistings. The principal tool is the wheel (figs. 8 and 10) by which threads attached to the small spools (shown in detail in fig.6) arranged at the top can be twisted, using the gearing of the two wheels A and B. Figs. 13 and 14 are the hooks which the twisted cords are wound round, at a distance from the wheel; figs. 3 and 12 are additional gearings for the wheels. Fig.1 shows a way of twisting from the creel (A).

Fig.11 shows a template which is incorporated into the weaving to make the curves of a fringe; it can be either cut out or slid out. This system is time-consuming and better

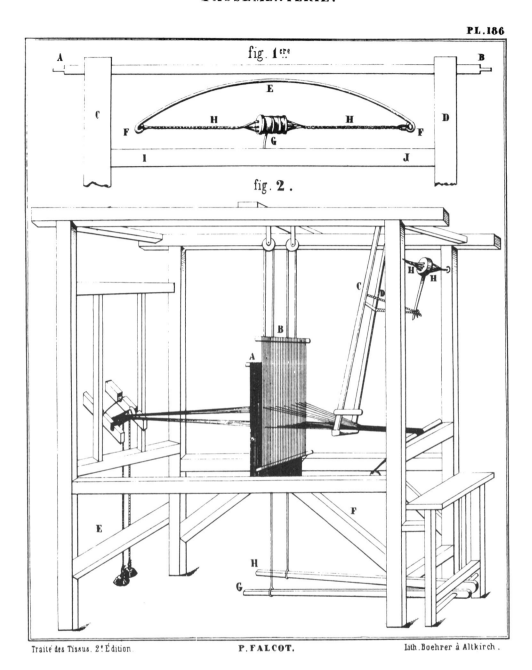

fig. 1ère

fig. 2.

Traité des Tissus. 2!Édition.   P.FALCOT.   Lith.Boehrer à Altkirch.

replaced by a series of metal threads as shown in figs. 2 and 4, whereby the weft works round the threads as required to give the graduated edge. After weaving, the looped ends of the fringe are twisted together (using the hook shown in fig.7) as shown in fig.9.

Fig.5 shows a three-bobbin shuttle for figured braids – see Plates 187 and 188.

Plate 186 illustrates a loom for making fringes. The loom is a normal one; note the cross-beams (F) to strengthen it (fig.2). The batten is held against the fabric by means of a spring for speed of working.

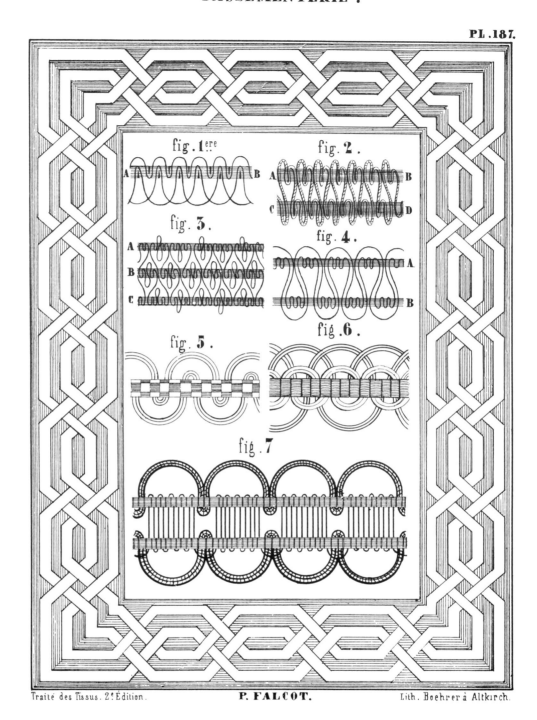

Traité des Tissus. 2ᵉ Édition. **P. FALCOT.** Lith. Boehrer à Altkirch.

Plate 187 This plate and Plate 188 show some variations of the thousands of *passementerie* designs possible, using one (fig.2), two (fig.4) or three (fig.5) shuttles; in some cases (fig.5) the shuttles have two or more bobbins in them.

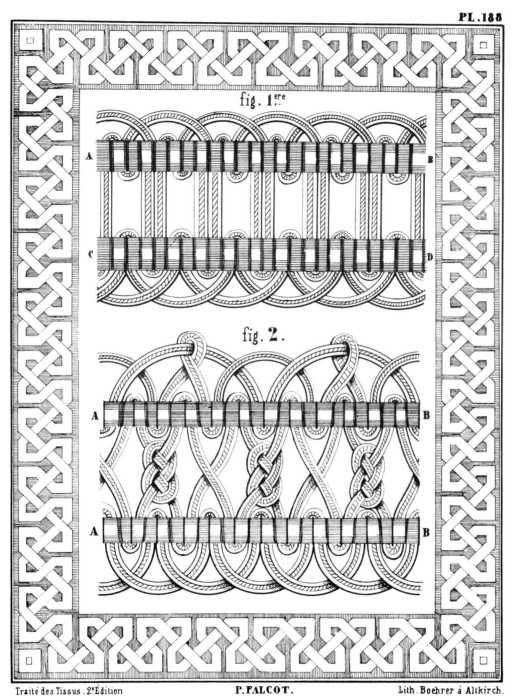

fig. 1.ere

fig. 2.

Traité des Tissus. 2ᵉÉdition   **P. FALCOT.**   Lith. Boehrer à Altkirch.

Plate 188 The numbers of shuttles and bobbins used in these examples can be worked out by inspection. Fig.2 is one of the most difficult of designs, because of the complicated alignment of shuttles.

ANCIEN MÉTIER À LA TIRE.

Pour étoffes façonnées, à Sample.

94

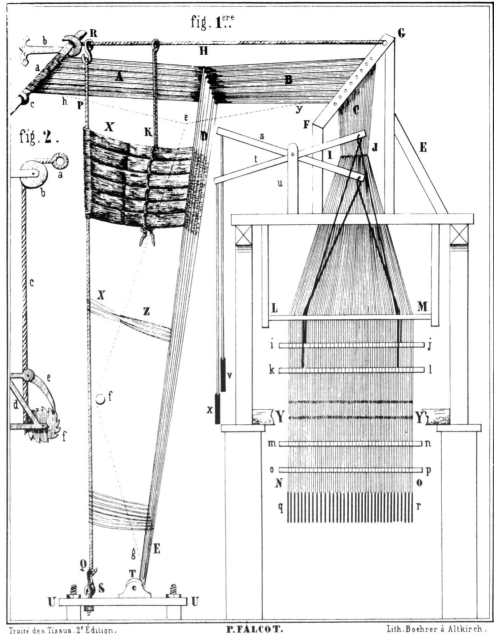

Traité des Tissus. 2ᵉ Édition.   P. FALCOT.   Lith. Boehrer à Altkirch.

Plate 190 shows an old draw loom. These were once used for all patterned fabric, but by Falcot's day had been made virtually obsolete by the Jacquard loom.

The main principles of the loom can be recognized from the looms already described. All the mails are suspended individually on weighted cords from the cords A–B which are suspended from the heavy rod (a). This latter can be fixed in brackets on the wall as shown in fig.1; or by means of a rope (fig.2) which allows for the height of the whole harness to be adjusted if necessary.

The design is woven into the simple cords (D), much as shown in Plate 96. Each pick is obtained by pulling the relevant cords attached to the pattern, shown (X–Z). This pulls back the cords (D), and hence those at A–B–C, to the angles shown by the dotted lines, and makes the shed. As can be seen, for a large design there will be a tight and confusing bundle of simple cords at the back of the loom.

MÉTIER À BOUTONS,
Ancien Système pour les étoffes façonnées.

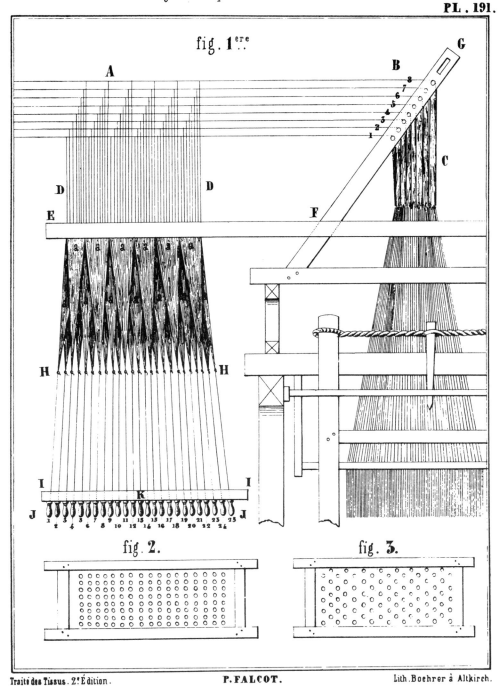

fig. 1ᵉʳᵉ

fig. 2.

fig. 3.

Traité des Tissus . 2ᵉ Édition .　　　P. FALCOT.　　　Lith.Boehrer à Altkirch.

Plate 191 shows the button loom which works on the same principle as the draw loom, except that it is operated by pulling handles which have the cords controlling the shed fixed to them; they are held in a wooden grid plate as shown in fig.3. There is no woven simple; the threads are attached directly to the cords in bunches. There is a disadvantage in the loss of the total flexibility of the draw loom but there is convenience in having just the handles to pull in sequence; some flexibility is allowed through pulling two handles at once to give another shed.

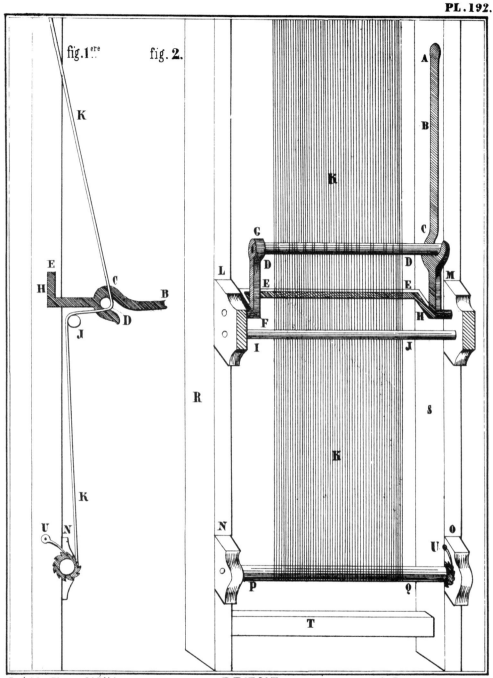

fig.1ere fig. 2.

Traité des Tissus. 2e Édition .   **P. FALCOT .**   Lith .Boehrer à Altkirch .

Plate 192 'A great boon for humanity' is how Falcot describes the invention of this drawing mechanism. The bar (D) is inserted behind the control cords at the back of the loom, pick by pick, and the cords are then pulled by using the lever (A–B–C). The raised warp threads, with their weights, could be very heavy, so this device greatly helped the draw boy by reducing the physical effort required.

The disadvantage of draw looms is the time taken to set them up; every new design needed new threading and tying, which left the weaver and draw boy with nothing to do. With the Jacquard, simply changing the cards allows for the weaving of another design on the same warp.

MONTOIR À BARRES

pour les chaînes en grosses matières.

PL. 193.

Lith Boehrer à Altkirch.

P. FALCOT

Traité des Tissus 2ᵉ Edition.

Plate 193 shows the way a woollen warp is put on the loom, the method shown for silk in Plate 3 being unsuitable owing to the elasticity of the yarn. A wide warp would need two people to wind, two to hold the raddle, and one to hold the end of the warp.

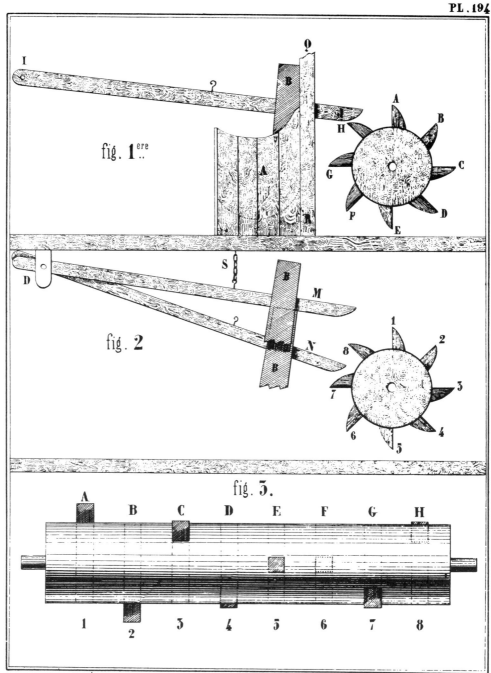

98

fig. 1ere..

fig. 2

fig. 3.

Traité des Tissus. 2.e Édition.   P. FALCOT.   Lith. Boehrer à Altkirch.

Plate 194 Falcot devotes many pages to the variety of finishing processes applied to woollen fabrics after weaving. (Silk needs little finishing, and cotton, because of its cheapness, does not warrant extensive and expensive finishing.)

This plate shows a machine for milling which felts the surface slightly and fills out the fibres. The fabric is rolled and put in the trough (A), which is filled with soapy water; sets of beaters arranged in pairs along its length rise as the cogs of the roller push them up and then fall back on to the cloth in a scissor-like action. The process is stopped at intervals to check the progress of the milling.

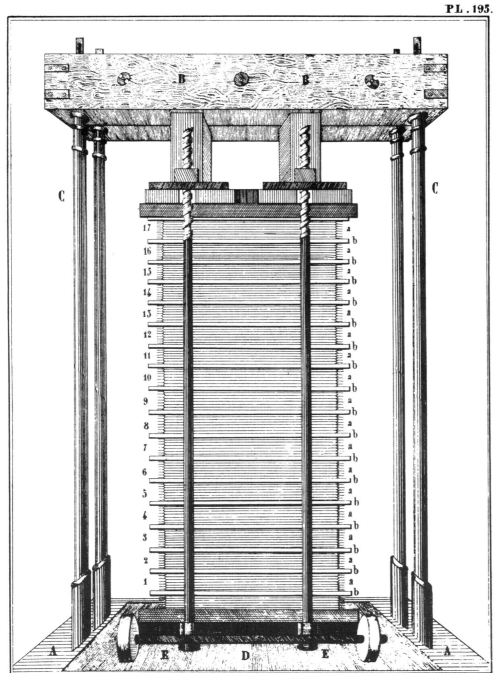

Traité des Tissus. 2.ᵉ Édition. **P. FALCOT.** Lith Boehrer à Altkirch.

Plate 195 shows the hot press, another part of the finishing process, which gave the cloth a soft and smooth appearance.

The cloth is folded in half lengthwise, then widthwise, with smooth card interleaved in the folds so that the cloth does not touch itself. Several lengths are placed on the platform with pairs of wooden boards between them; hot metal plates are then inserted between the boards and the whole pile wheeled under the press. It is held steady as the platform is screwed up into the press; after the necessary time, the press is undone and the fabric left to rest; after refolding, the process is repeated.

At a later stage, a cold pressing takes place (by the same method, but without the hot plates).

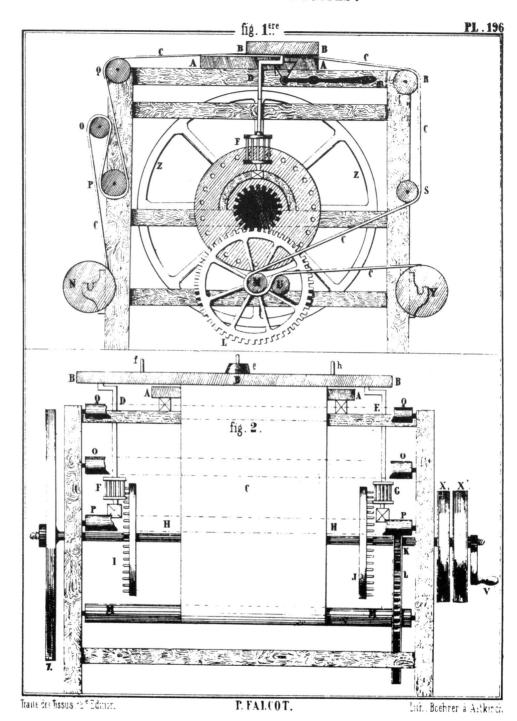

fig. 1ᵉʳᵉ

fig. 2.

Traité des Tissus 2ᵉ Edition.   P. FALCOT.   Lith. Boehrer à Altkirch.

Plate 196 shows a machine for giving a finish which will leave a circular surface pattern.

The cloth passes over the fixed platform (A), and is subjected to a circular rubbing by the top plate (B) which has a sandpaper surface. The machine is turned by the axle (H), which gears both the movement of the cloth and the circular movement of the top.

The passage of the cloth through the machine can be seen in fig.1; it is held in tension by the rollers. Care must be taken not to work too slowly, or the machine will rub holes in the fabric.

BATTANT BROCHEUR.

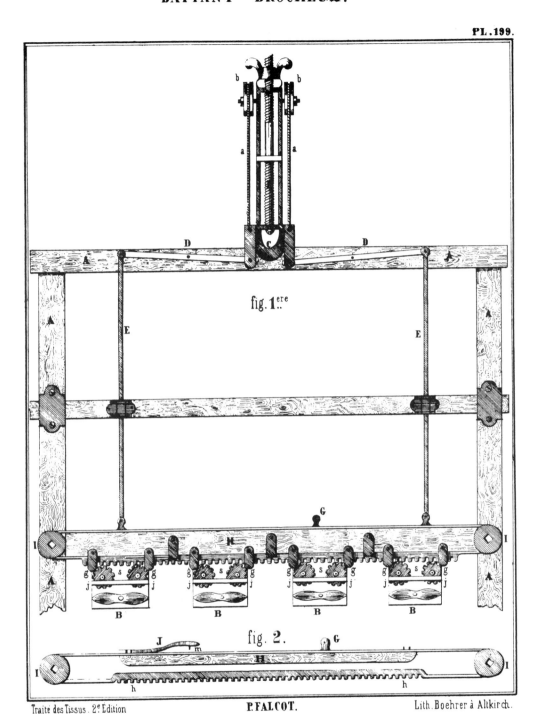

fig. 1.ère

fig. 2.

Traité des Tissus. 2.e Edition   P. FALCOT.   Lith. Boehrer à Altkirch.

Plate 199 shows a brocading batten, used where a brocade is made with several small shuttles in a single pass (see Plate 114). It allows for all the shuttles to be operated together.

There is an ordinary batten chassis, which also carries the bar with boxes (B) for the brocading shuttles. This part is usually kept above the weaving; it is lowered as programmed by the Jacquard punch card, and the shuttles are activated by pushing the handle (G) to right or left. The strong spring (F) lifts the batten back to its rest position after use.

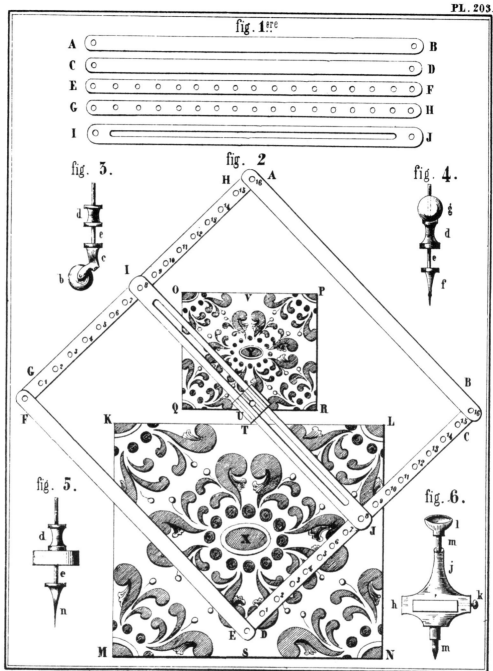

fig. 1ere

fig. 2

fig. 3.

fig. 4.

fig. 5.

fig. 6.

Traité des Tissus. 2ᵉ Édition.

P. FALCOT.

Lith. Boehrer à Altkirch.

Plate 203 illustrates a pantograph by means of which designs can be enlarged or reduced.

The five wooden pieces shown in fig.1 are assembled as shown in fig.2. The angle at A–H is joined at the weighted point (fig.4); G–F and B–C are on small wheels (fig.3); and E–D is the blunt tracing point (fig.5). Fig.6 shows the pencil holder at U, adjustable along the slotted piece I–J. As it moves towards G–H the design reduces, towards C–D it enlarges. The positioning of the bar I–J also affects the proportion of the reproduced design.

MACHINE à reproduire les Dessins par M. GRILLET. PL. 208.

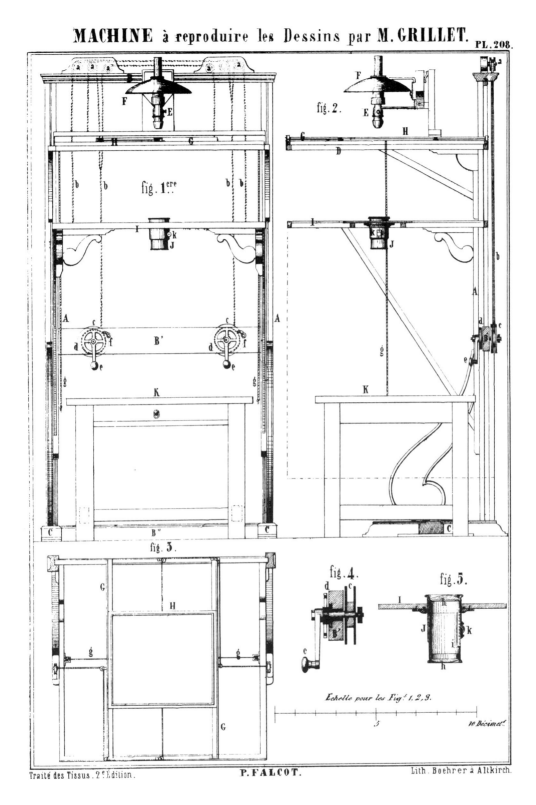

fig. 1ᵉʳᵉ.

fig. 2.

fig. 3.

fig. 4.

fig. 5.

Échelle pour les Figˢ 1, 2, 3.

5   10 Décimet.

Traité des Tissus. 2ᵉ Édition.   P. FALCOT.   Lith. Boehrer à Altkirch.

Plate 208 shows the enlarger, a most ingenious machine for reproducing, enlarging or reducing designs. It has the advantage over the pantograph of allowing the exact size of the image to be seen before the copy is drawn.

Light shines from the lamp (F) through the original design which is on glass; the image is focused through the lens (J) on to paper placed on the table (K), where it can be drawn. The image can be focused to the size desired by adjustment of the height of the lens or the table, by means of the chains shown (b). The frame can be moved laterally (seen from above in fig.3), so that all parts of the design can be centred. The image reduces as the lens is moved towards the table.

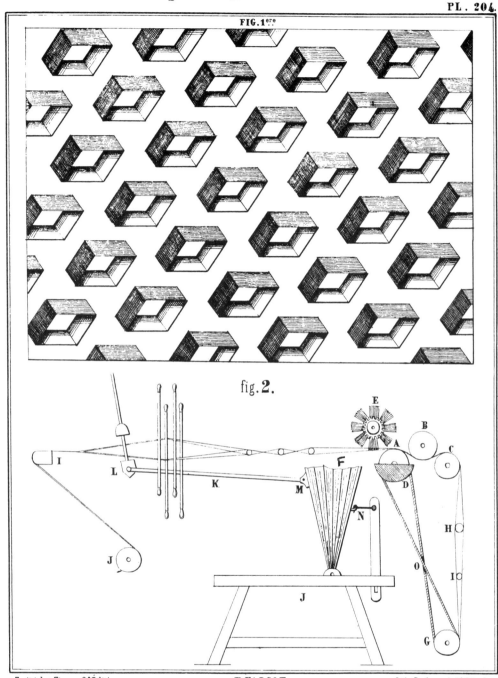

FIG.1ère

fig.2.

Traité des Tissus. 2e Édition. **P. FALCOT.** Lith. Boehrer à Altkirch.

Plate 204 shows (in fig.2), a mechanism for continuous sizing and drying of a linen or cotton warp. The usual method of sizing required the weaver to apply the size by hand, resulting in loss of weaving time through stopping work and waiting for the size to dry. Here, a trough (D) holding the size is placed across the back of the loom. It contains a roller (A) over which the warp passes. The brush (E) smoothes over the wet warp, while the bellows (F), controlled by the movement of the batten (L), dries the warp.

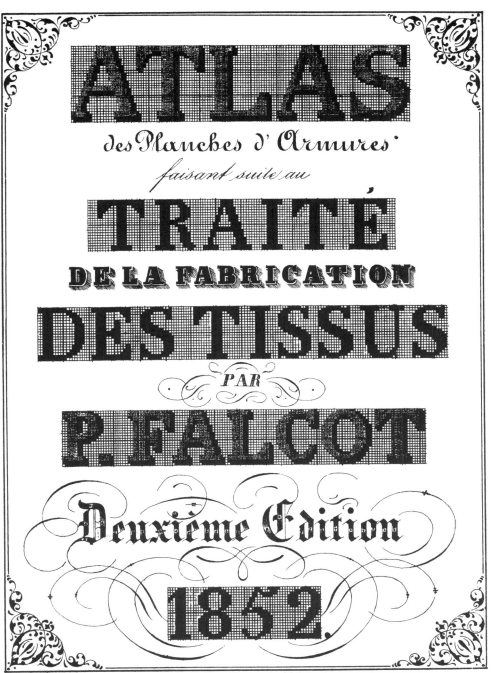

ATLAS

des Planches d'Armures

faisant suite au

TRAITÉ

DE LA FABRICATION

DES TISSUS

PAR

P. FALCOT

Deuxième Edition

1852.

Lith. B. Boehrer à Altkirch.

109

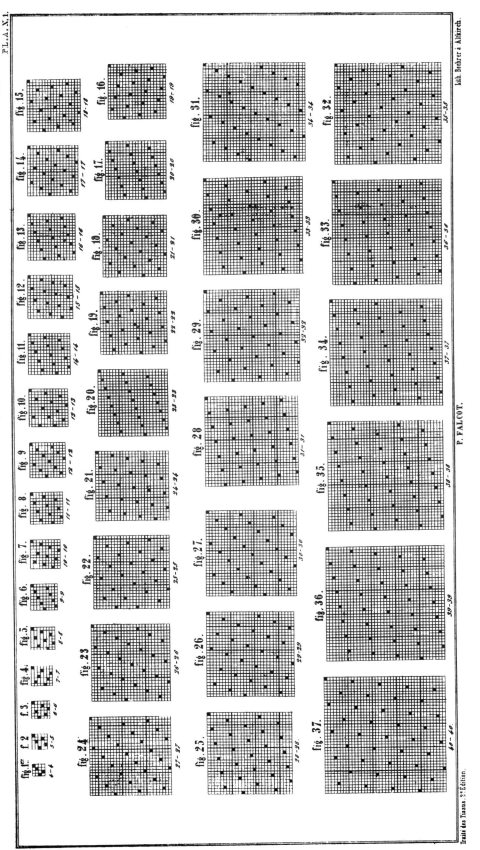

TABLEAU SYNOPTIQUE,

Servant à la formation des croisements dits Armures ou Petits Façonnés, depuis quatre jusqu'a quarante inclusivement

P. FALCOT.

4 Sur 4.

4 Sur 6.

4 Sur 8.

4 Sur 12.

4 Sur 16.

4 Sur 20.

Traité des Tissus. 2.ᵉ Edition.   P. FALCOT.   Lith. Boehrer à Altkirch.

ARMURES DIVERSES.

5 Sur 5.

5 Sur 10.

5 Sur 15.

5 Sur 20.

5 Sur 25.

Traité des Tissus. 2.ᵉ Édition.   P. FALCOT.   Lith. Boehrer à Altkirch.

6 Sur 6.

6 Sur 8.

6 Sur 10.

6 Sur 12.

6 Sur 18.

ARMURES DIVERSES.

7 Sur 7.

7 Sur 14.

7 Sur 21.

7 Sur 28.

Traité des Tissus. 2.ᵉ Édition   P. FALCOT.   Lith. Boehrer à Altkirch.

8 sur 8.

P. FALCOT.

8 Sur 12.

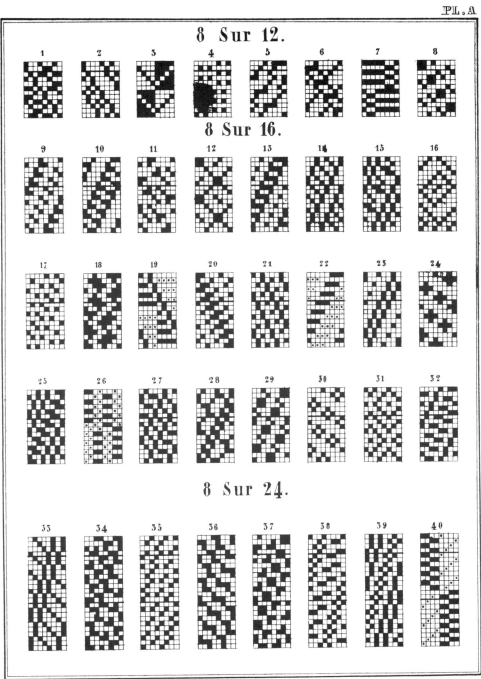

8 Sur 16.

8 Sur 24.

9 Sur 9.

9 Sur 18.

9 Sur 27.

ARMURES DIVERSES.

10 sur 10.

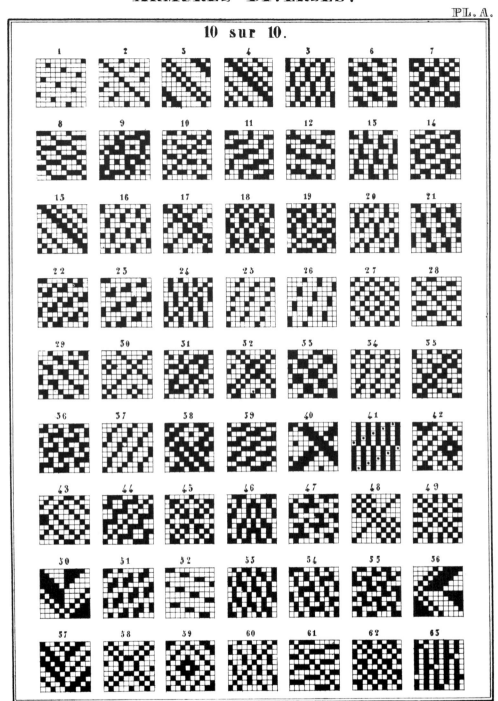

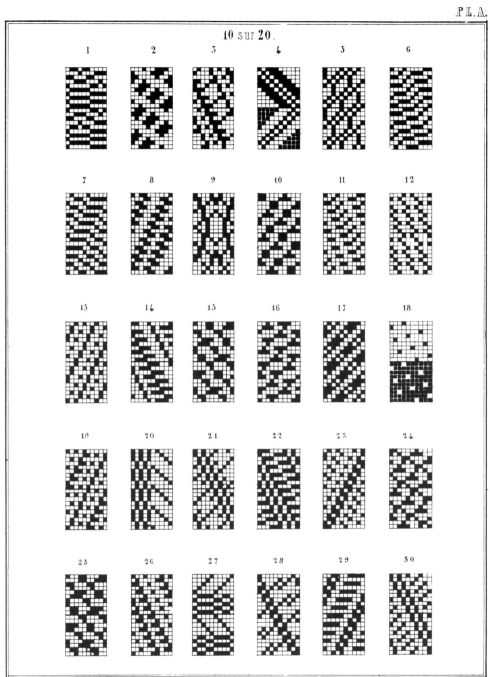

10 sur 20 .

P. FALCOT.

ARMURES DIVERSES.

10 sur 20.

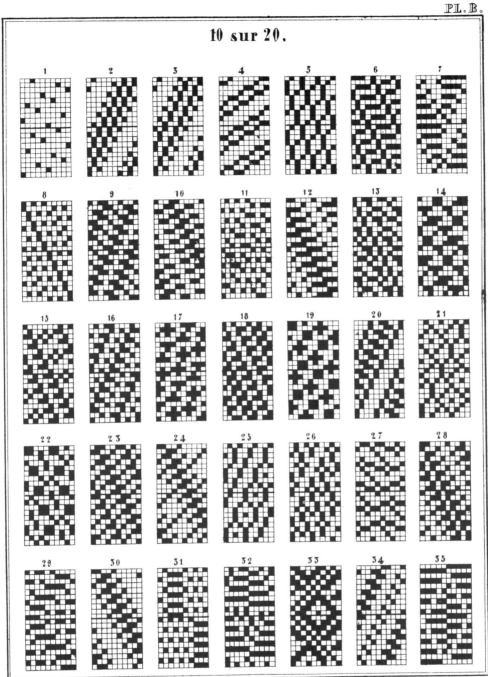

ARMURES DIVERSES.

10 sur 30.

Traité des Tissus. 2ᵉ Edition.   **P. FALCOT.**   Lith. Boehrer à Altkirch.

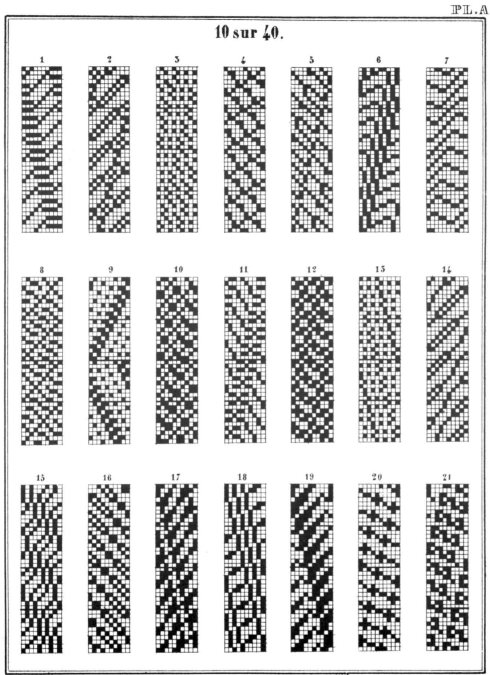

10 sur 40.

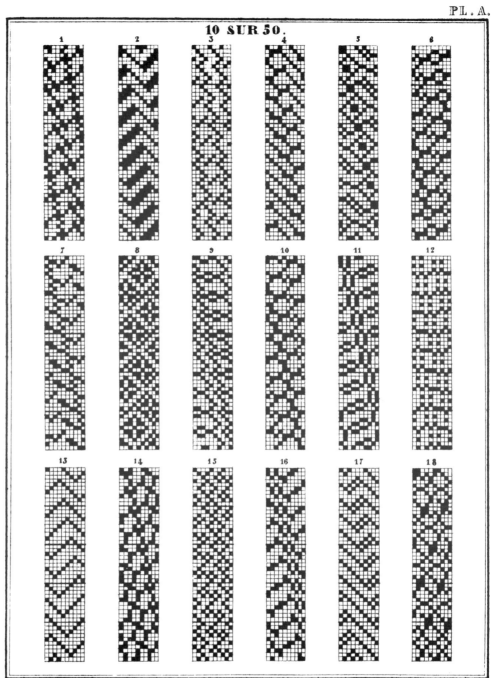

10 SUR 50.

P. FALCOT.

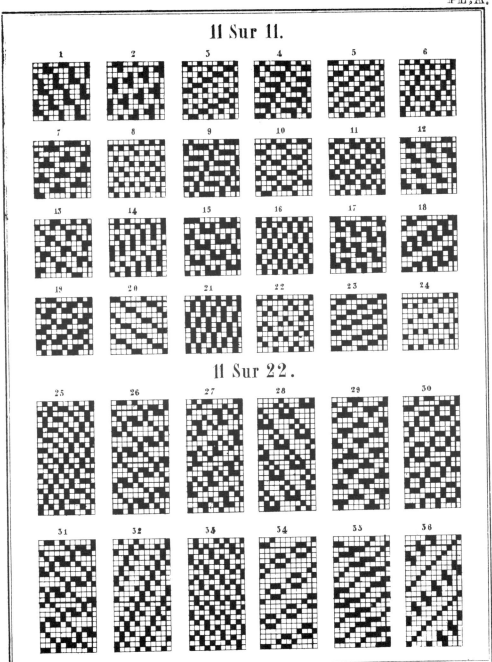

11 Sur 11.

11 Sur 22.

Traité des Tissus. 2.ᵉ Édition.   **P.FALCOT.**   Lith. Boehrer à Altkirch.

11 Sur 11.

11 Sur 22.

Traité des Tissus. 2.ᵉ Édition.   **P. FALCOT.**   Lith. Boehrer à Altkirch.

12 sur 12.

Traité des Tissus. 2ᵉ Édition   P. FALCOT.   Lith. Boehrer à Altkirch.

12 Sur 24.

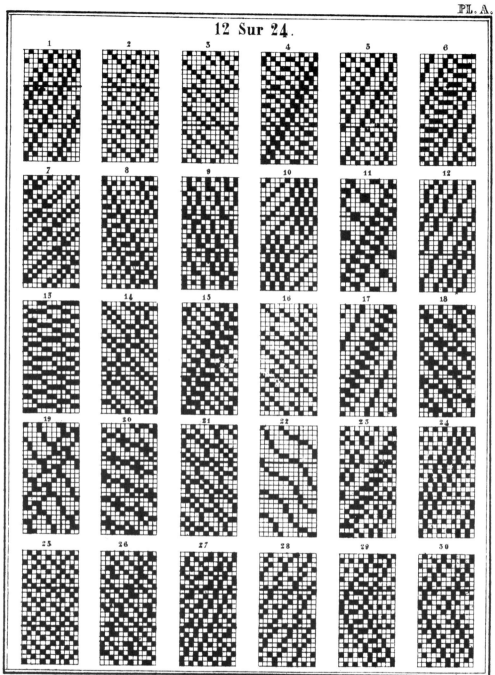

P. FALCOT.

12 Sur 24.

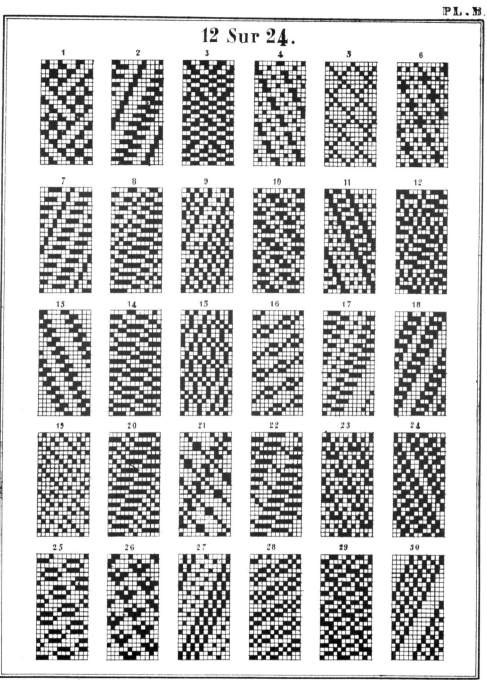

Traité des Tissus. 2.ᵉ Édition.   P. FALCOT.   Lith. Boehrer à Altkirch.

12 Sur 36.

P. FALCOT

Lith. Boehrer à Altkirch.

13 Sur 13.

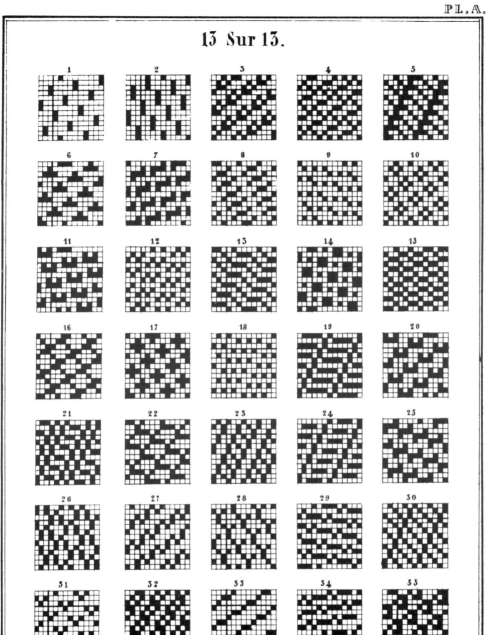

Traité des Tissus. 2.ᵉ Édition.　　　　P. FALCOT.　　　　Lith. Bœhrer à Altkirch.

13 Sur 26.

1   2   3   4   5

6   7   8   9   10

11   12   13   14   15

16   17   18   19   20

Traité des Tissus. 2.ᵉ Édition.   P. FALCOT.   Lith. Boehrer à Altkirch.

14 Sur 14.

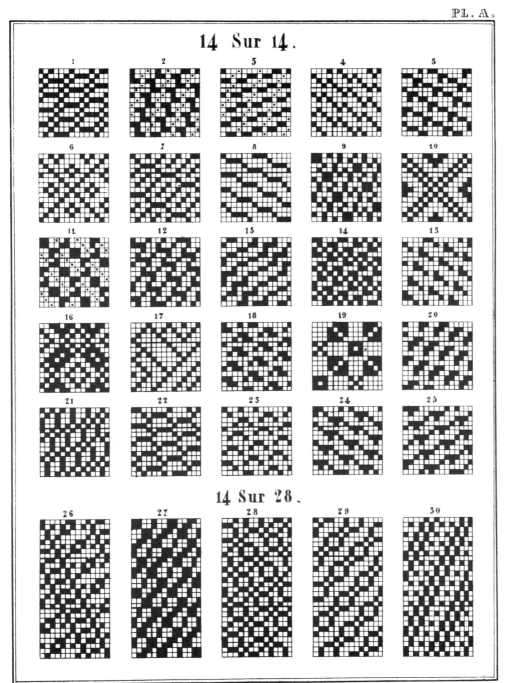

14 Sur 28.

15 sur 15.

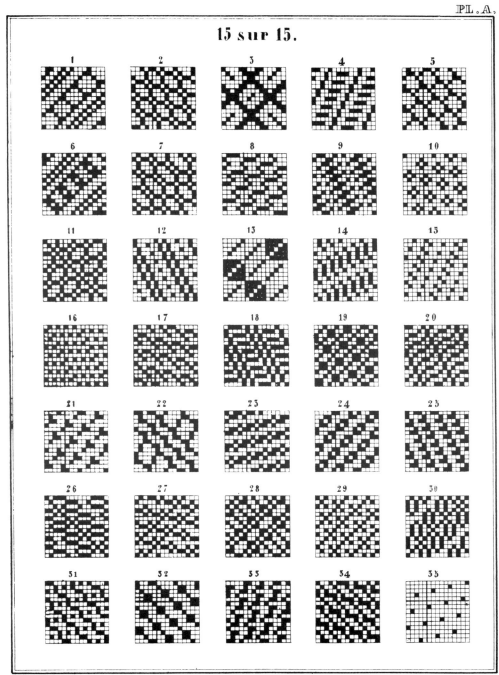

ARMURES DIVERSES.

15 sur 15.

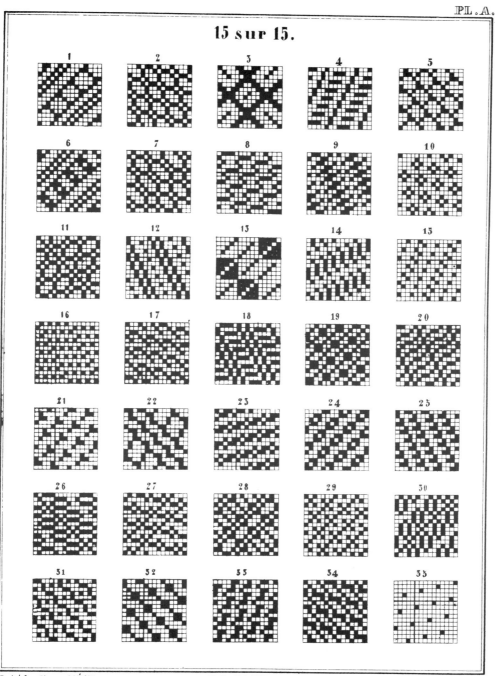

15 Sur 30.

P. FALCOT. Lith. Boehrer à Altkirch.

ARMURES DIVERSES.

16 sur 16.

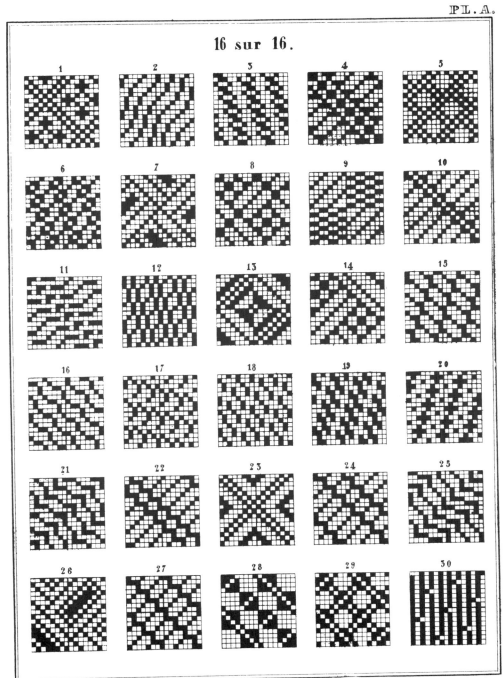

Traité des Tissus. 2.° Édition.   P. FALCOT.   Lith. Boehrer à Altkirch.

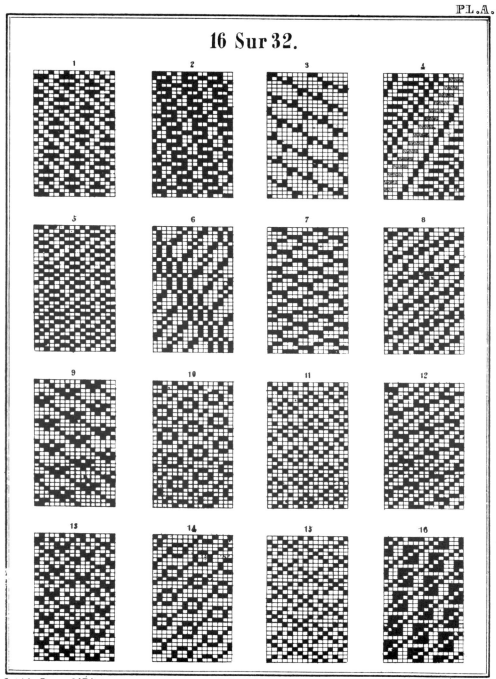

ARMURES DIVERSES.

16 Sur 32.

P. FALCOT.

17 Sur 17.

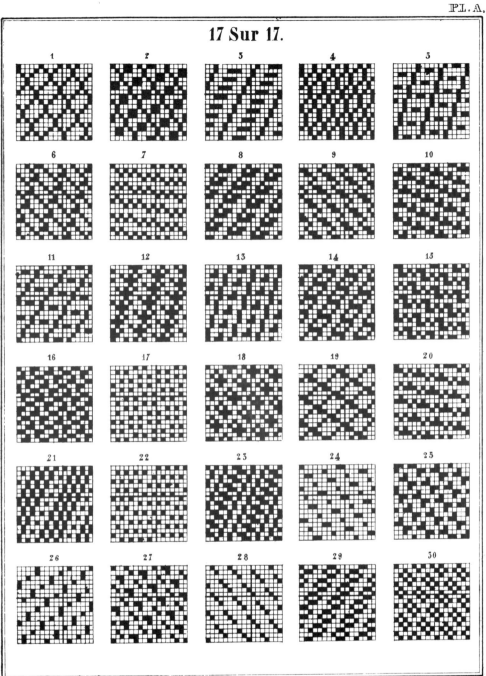

17 Sur 17.

17 Sur 34.

ARMURES DIVERSES.

18 Sur 18.

18 Sur 18.

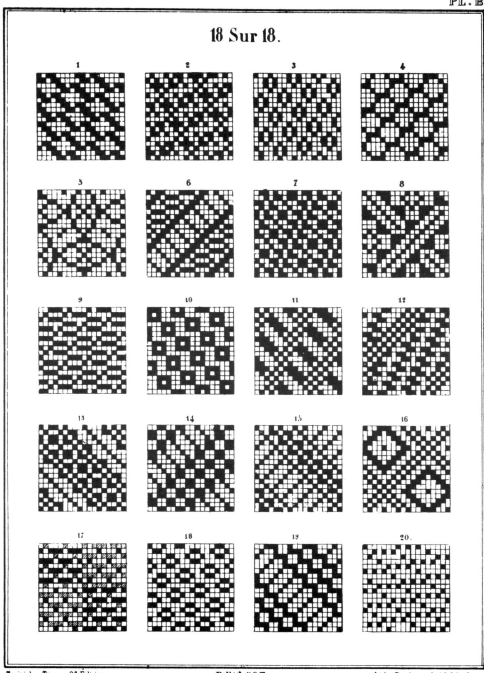

19 Sur 19.

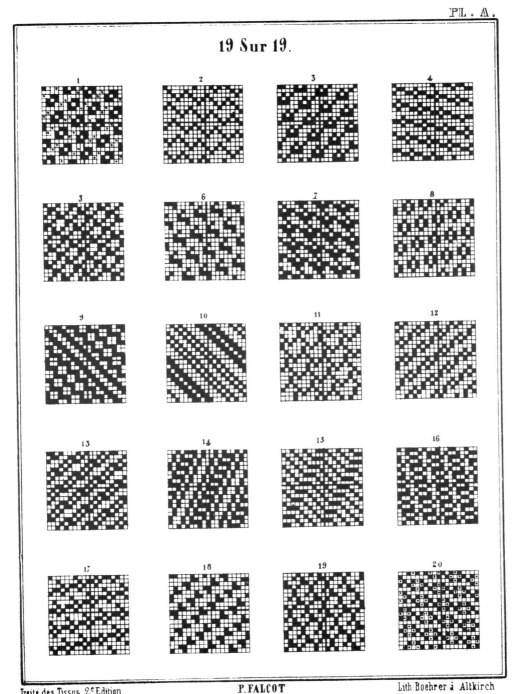

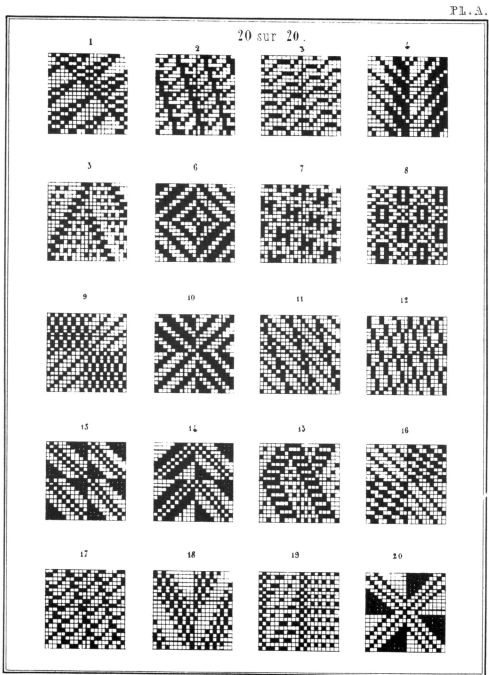

20 sur 20.

20 Sur 20.

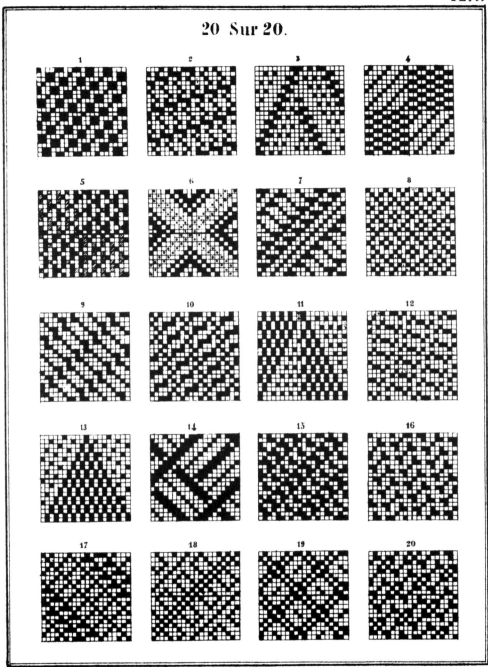

20 Sur 20.

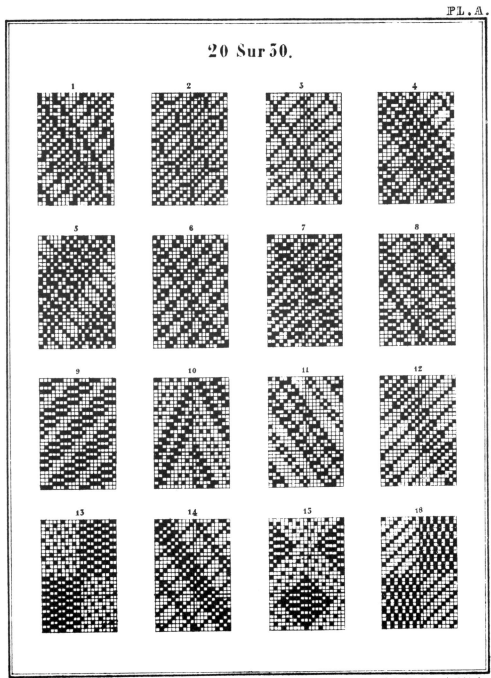

20 Sur 30.

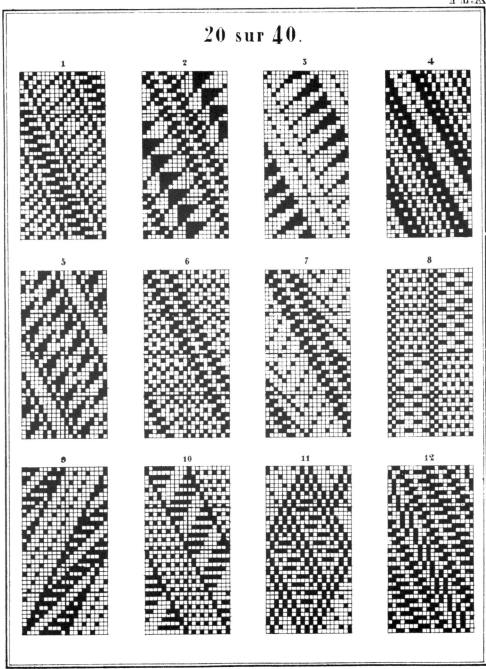

20 sur 40.

20 sur 40.

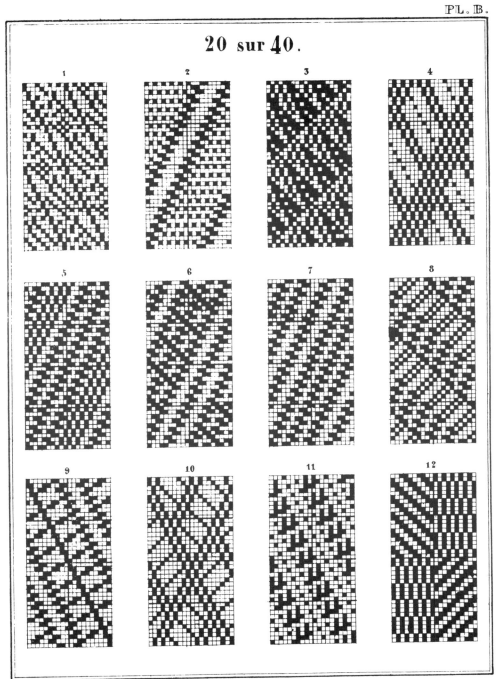

148

20 Sur 40.

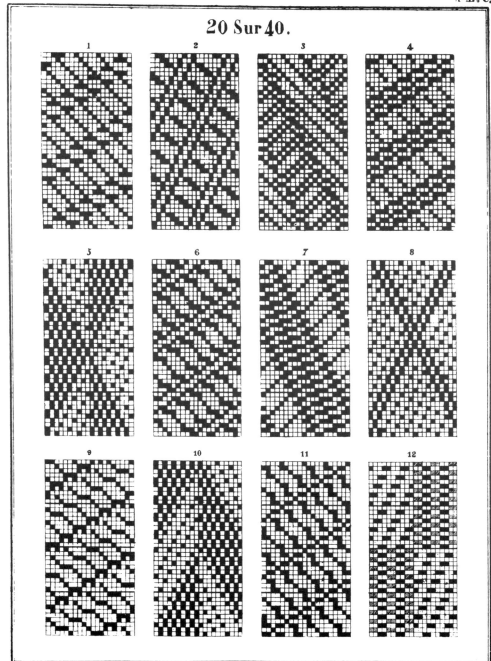

ARMURES DIVERSES.

21 Sur 21.

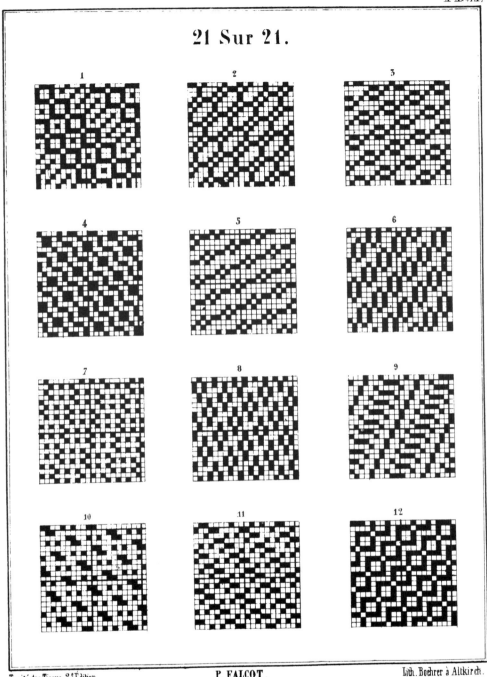

P. FALCOT.

Lith. Boehrer à Altkirch.

21 Sur 21.

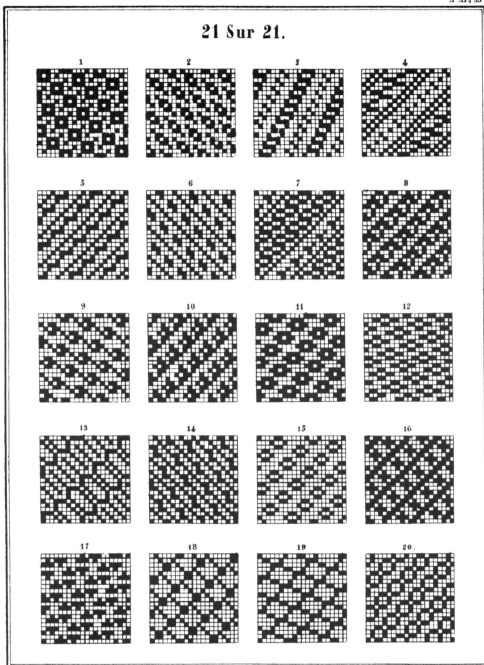

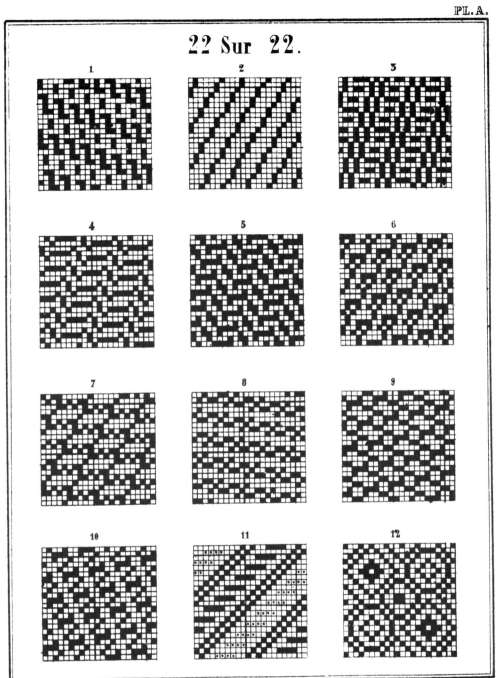

22 Sur 22.

P. FALCOT.

152

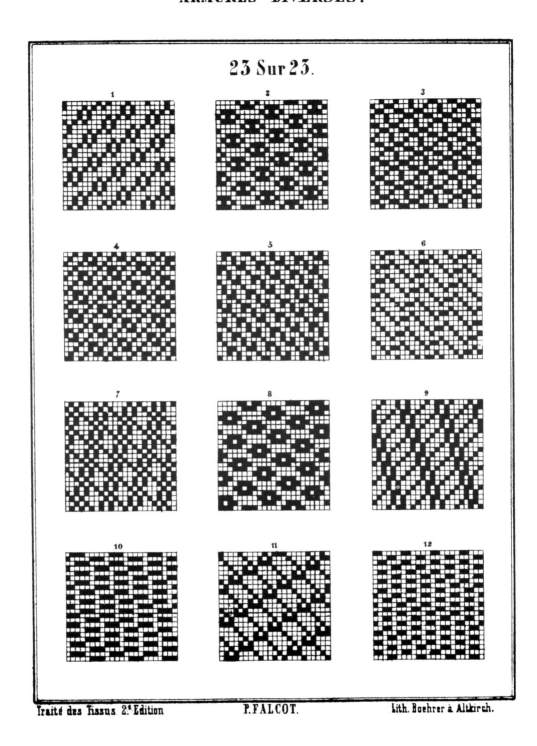

23 Sur 23.

24 Sur 24.

24 Sur 24.

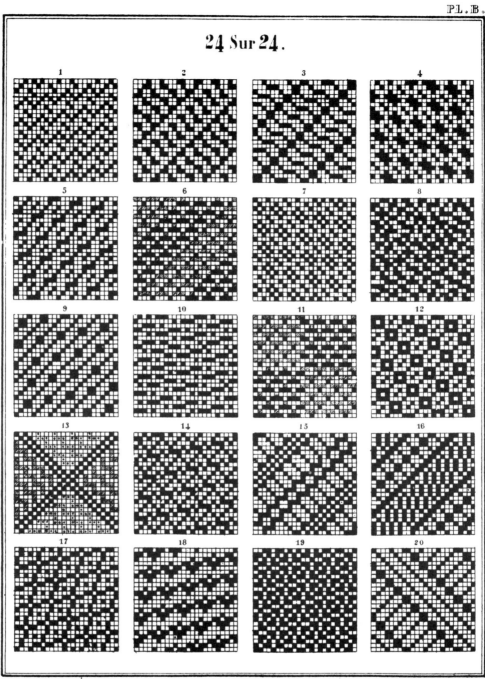

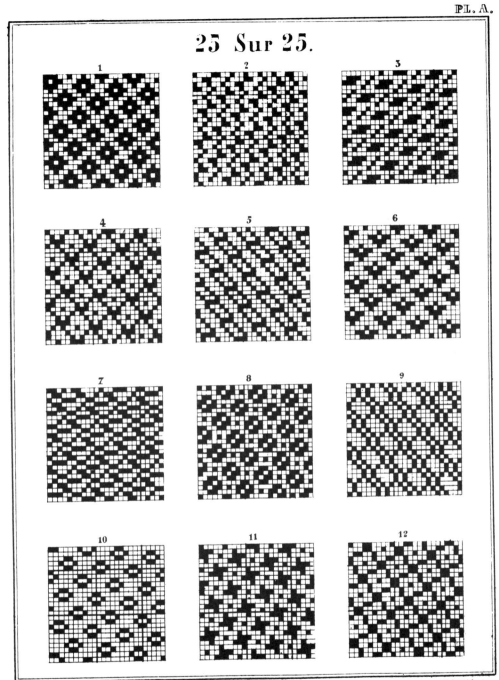

25 Sur 25.

26 Sur 26.

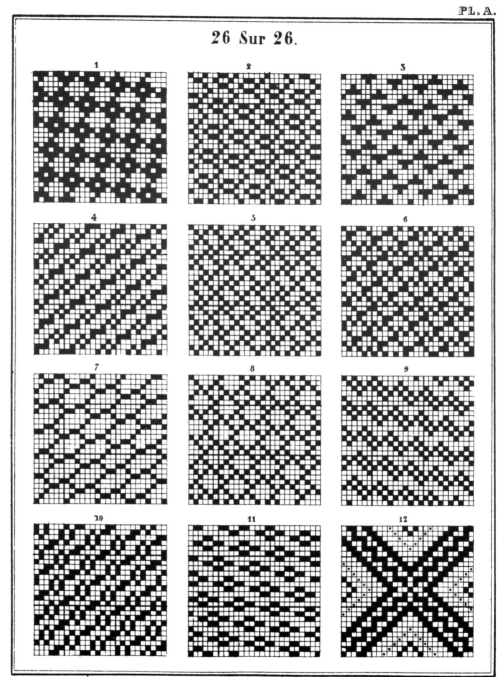

27 Sur 27.

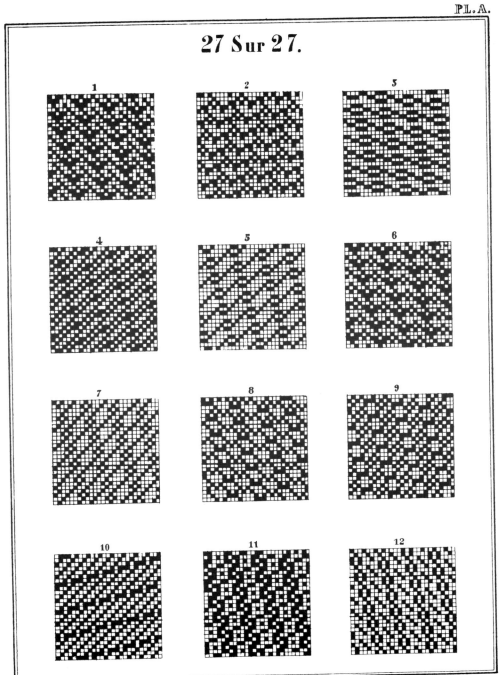

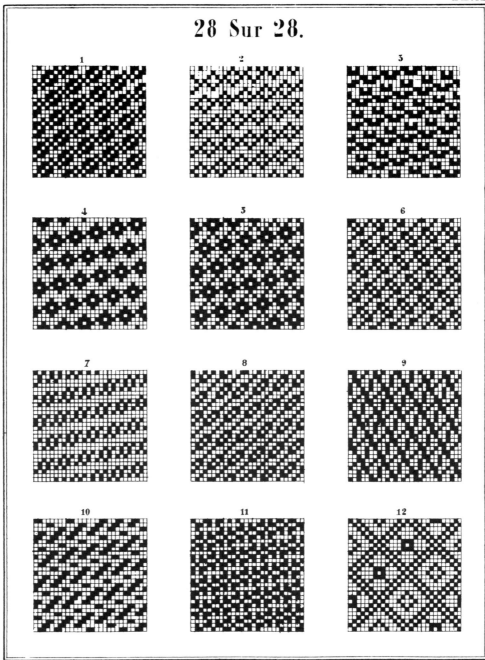

28 Sur 28.

ARMURES DIVERSES.

29 Sur 29.

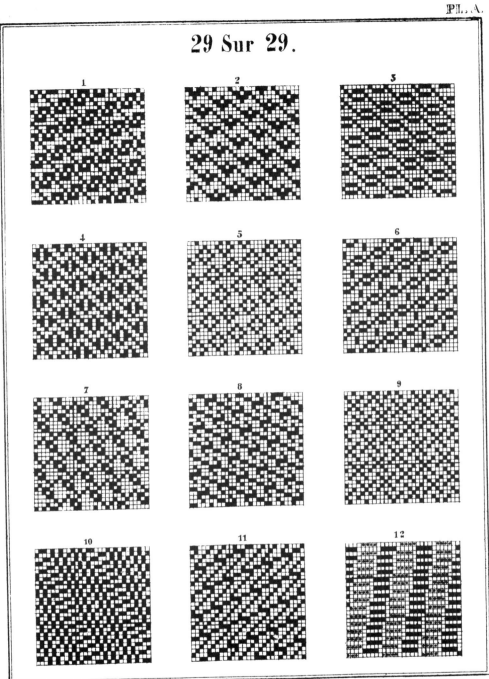

Traité des Tissus. 2ᵉ Édition   P. FALCOT.   Lith. Boehrer à Altkirch.

30 sur 30.

30 Sur 30.

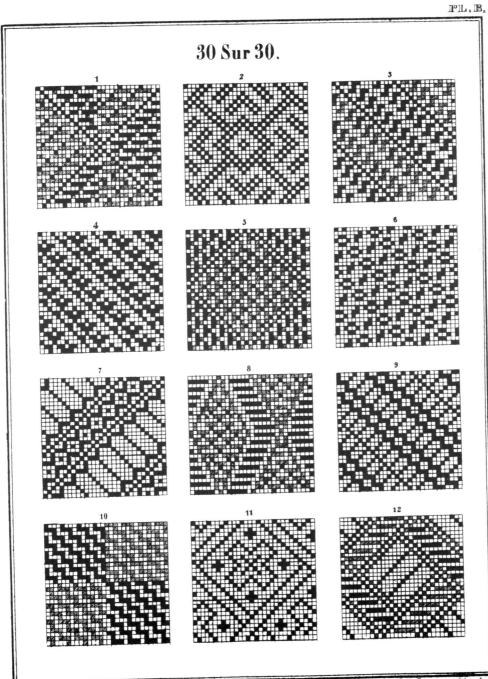

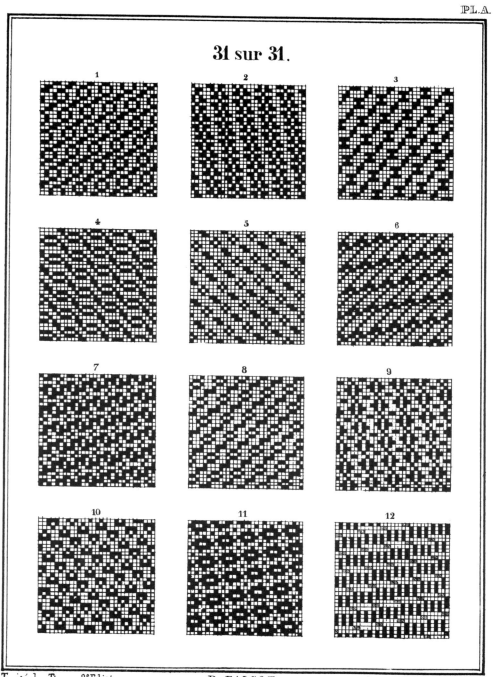

31 sur 31.

ARMURES DIVERSES.

32 Sur 32.

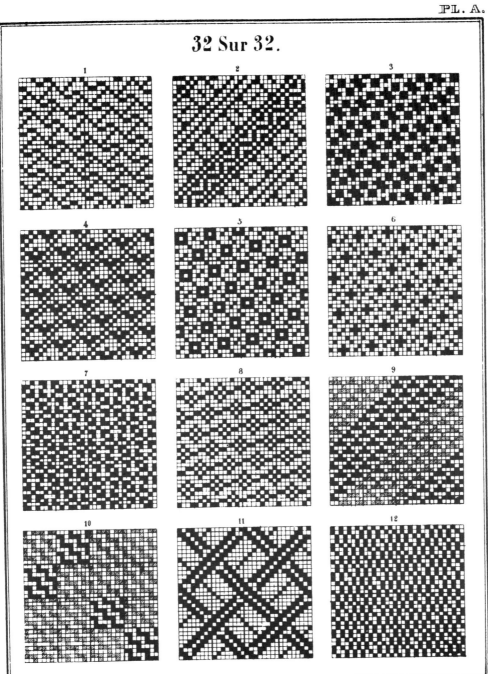

32 sur 32.

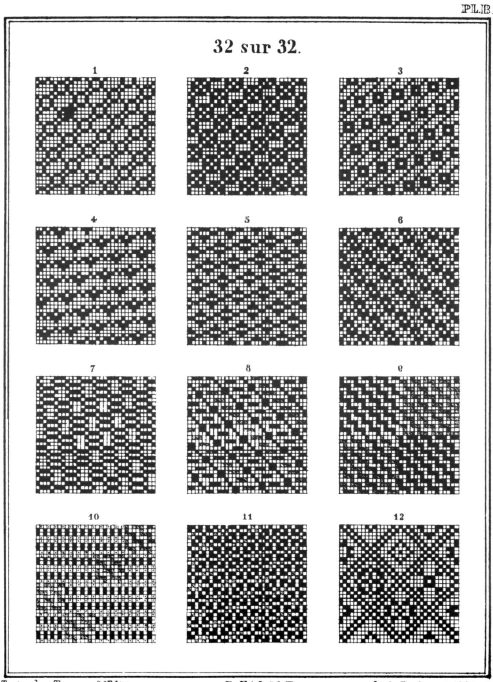

P. FALCOT.

ARMURES DIVERSES.

33 sur 33.

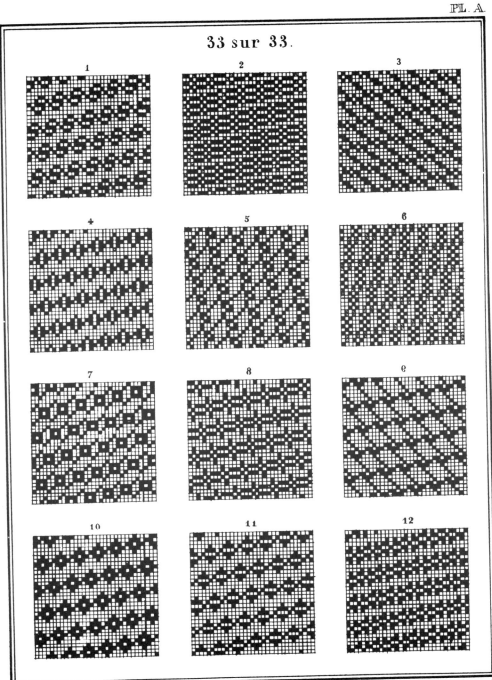

Traité des Tissus. 2ᵉ Edition.   P. FALCOT.   Lith. Boehrer à Altkirch.

35 sur 35.

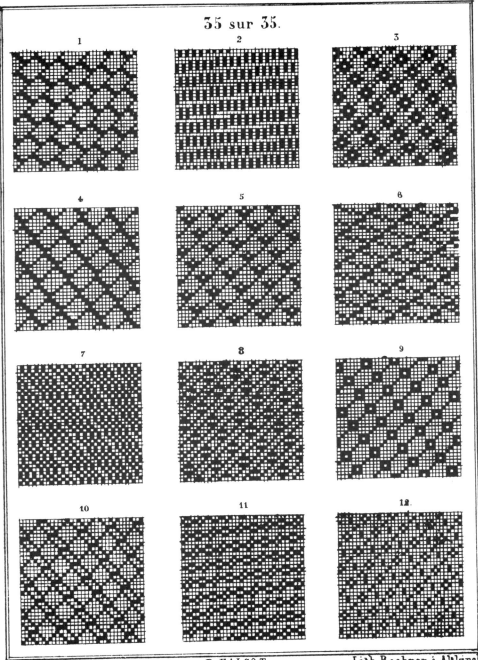

Traité des Tissus. 2.e Edition.   P. FALCOT.   Lith.Boehrer à Altkirch.

ARMURES DIVERSES.

168

36 sur 36.

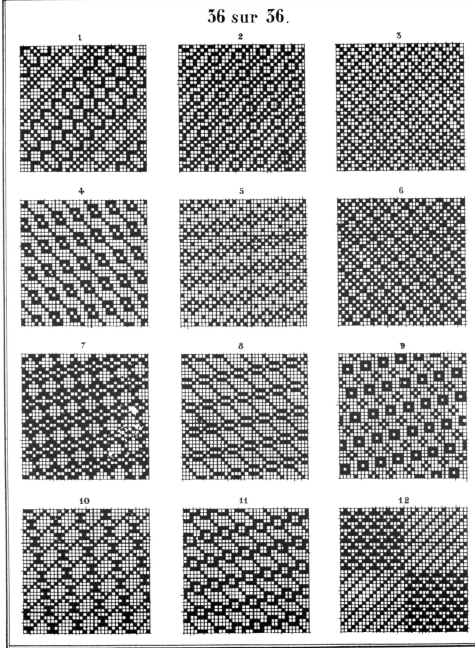

Traité des Tissus. 2.ᵉ Edition.   P FALCOT.   Lith Boehrer à Altkirch.

37 sur 37.

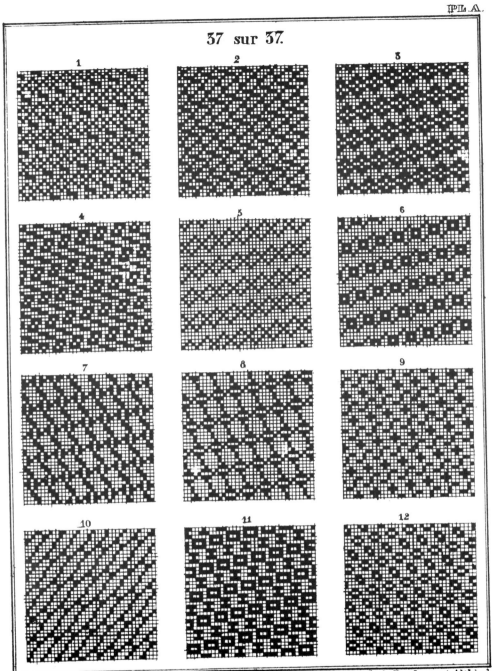

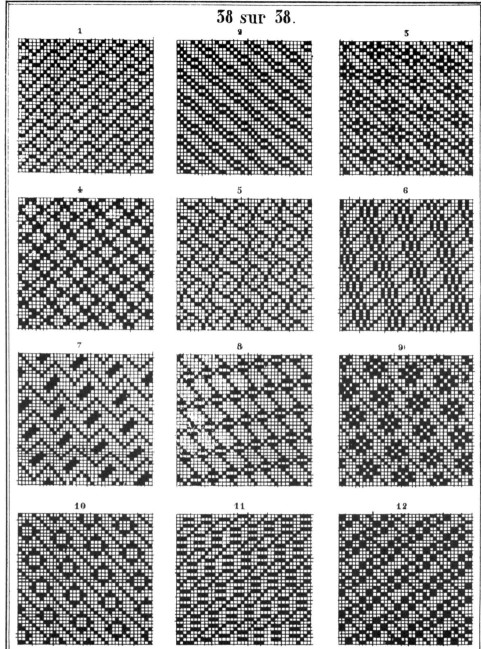

38 sur 38.

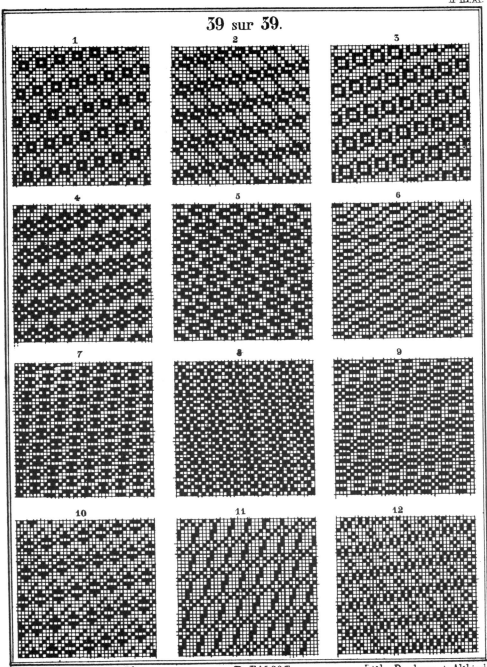

39 sur 39.

40 sur 40.

1   2

3   4

5   6

40 sur 40.

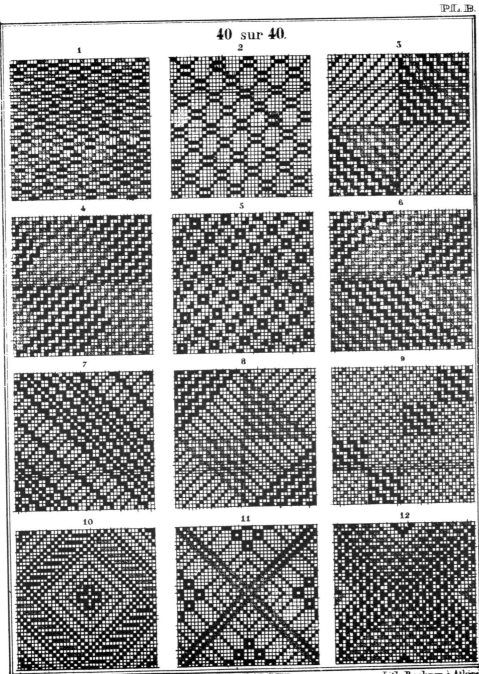

Traité des Tissus. 2.e Edition.   P. FALCOT.   Lith. Boehrer à Altkirch.

PL.A

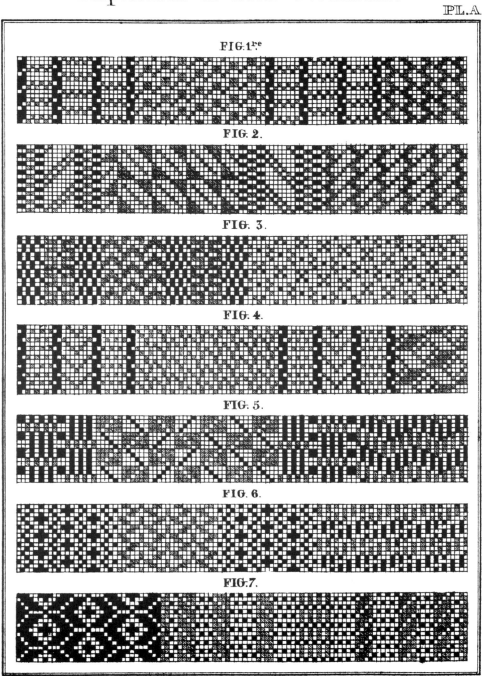

FIG:1.re

FIG. 2.

FIG. 3.

FIG. 4.

FIG. 5.

FIG. 6.

FIG:7.

PL. IB

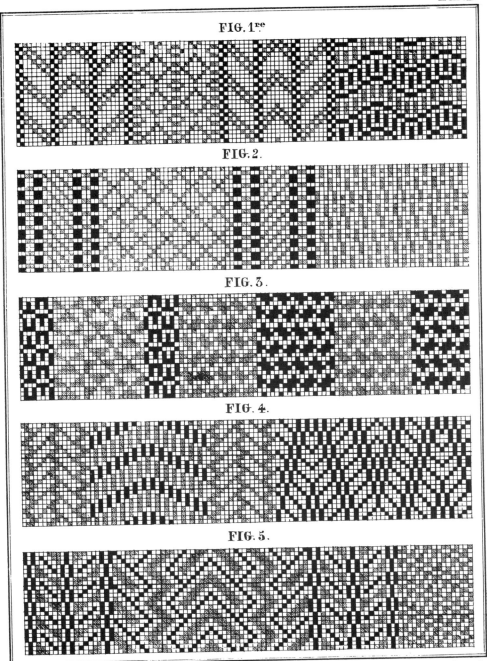

FIG. 1re

FIG. 2.

FIG. 3.

FIG. 4.

FIG. 5.

Traité des Tissus. 2e Édition.   P. FALCOT.   Lith. Boehrer à Altkirch.

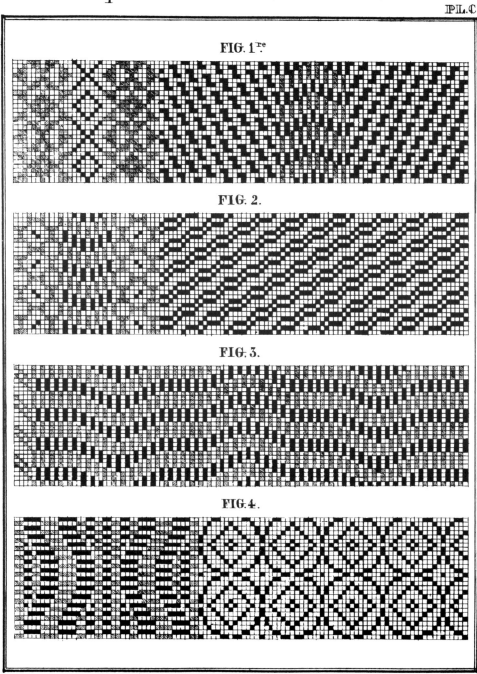

FIG. 1ʳᵉ

FIG. 2.

FIG. 3.

FIG. 4.

Traité des Tissus. 2ᵉ Edition.   P. FALCOT.   Lith. Boehrer à Altkirch.

BANDES & FILETS.

Dispositions diverses.– Documents.

PL. D

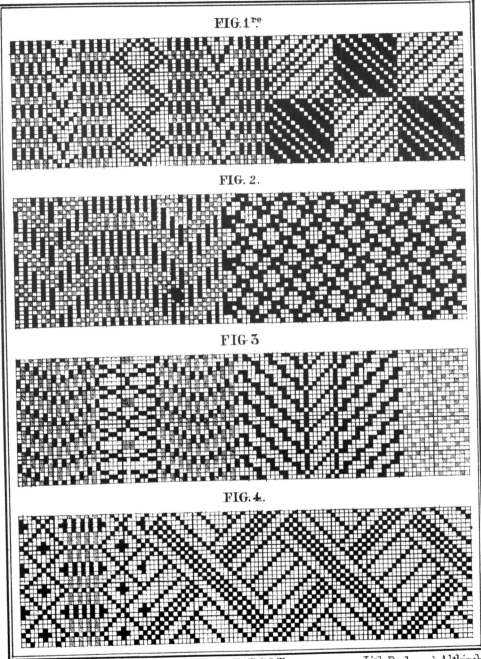

FIG. 1re

FIG. 2.

FIG 3

FIG. 4.

Traité des Tissus. 2e Edition.   P. FALCOT.   Lith. Boehrer à Altkirch.

BANDES & FILETS.

Dispositions diverses.—Documents.

fig. 1.ʳᵉ

fig. 2.

fig. 3.

fig. 4.

Traité des Tissus. 2.ᵉ Edition   P. FALCOT.   Lith. B. Boehrer à Altkirch.

PL.F.

fig.1re

fig.2.

fig.3.

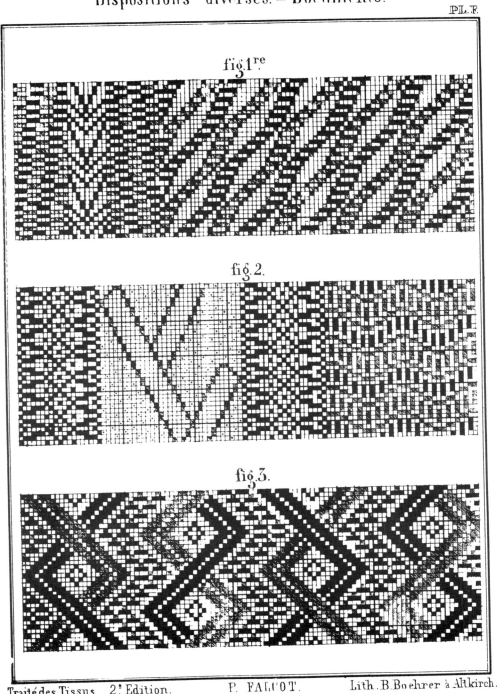

BANDES & FILETS.
Dispositions diverses.~Documents.

fig.1 re

fig.2.

fig.3.

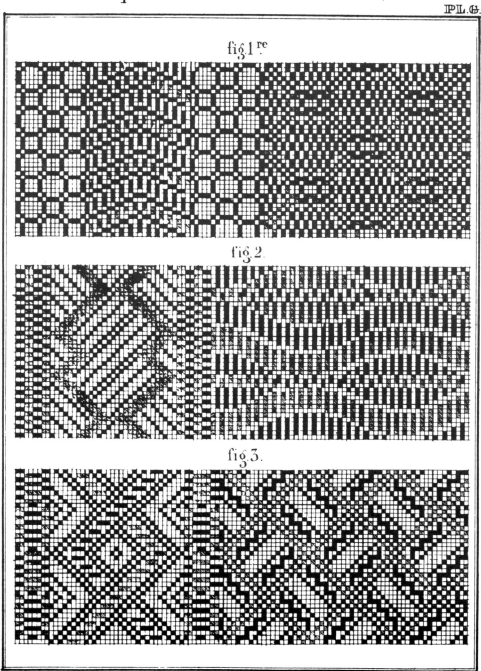

Traité des Tissus . 2.e Edition.   P. FALCOT.   Lith.B.Boehrer à Altkirch.

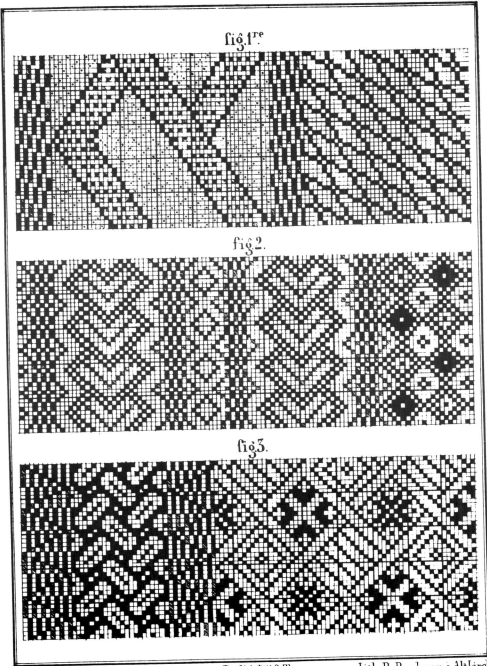

fig.1re

fig.2.

fig.3.

ARMURES DIVERSES
pour fonds, bandes, filets. ~ Documents.

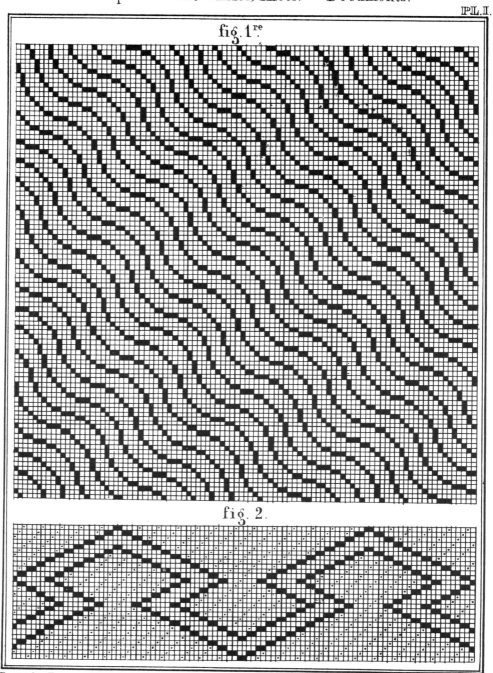

fig. 1.re

fig. 2.

Traité des Tissus. 2.e Edition.   P. FALCOT.   Lith. Boehrer à Altkirch.

ARMURES DIVERSES

pour fonds, bandes, filets. – Documents.

PL. 1.

fig. 1re

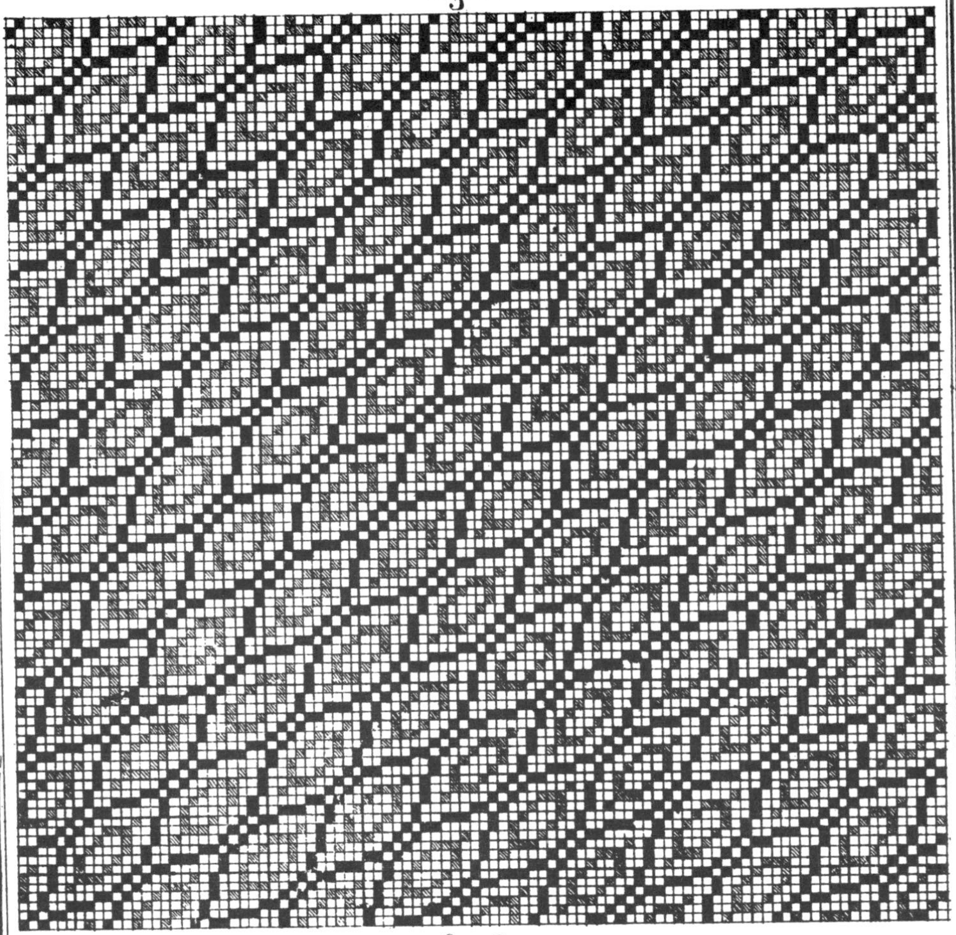

fig. 2

Traité des Tissus. 2e Edition.　　　P. FALCOT.　　　Lith. Boehrer à Altkirch.

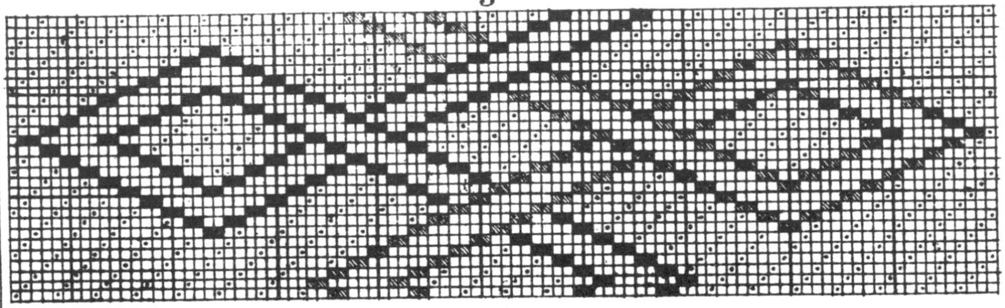

ARMURES DIVERSES
pour fonds, bandes, filets. – Documents.

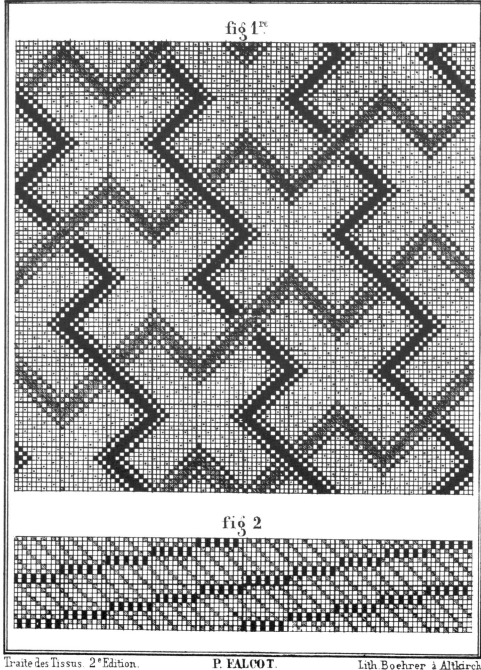

fig 1re

fig 2

Traité des Tissus. 2e Edition.   P. FALCOT.   Lith.Boehrer à Altkirch.

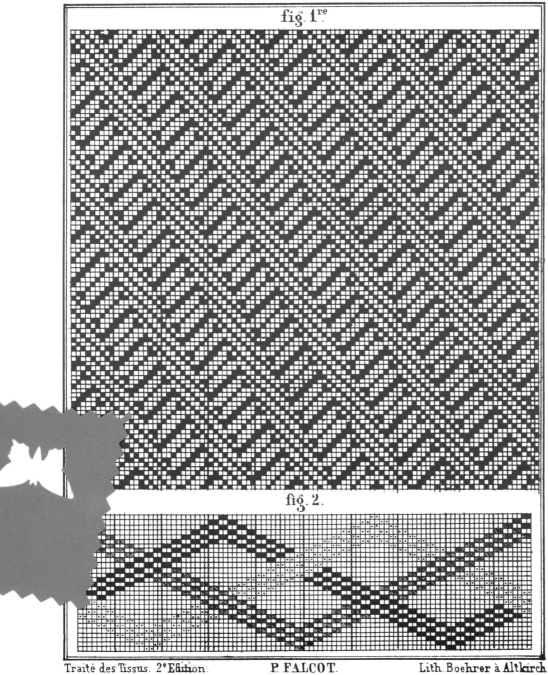

fig. 1re.

fig. 2.

ARMURES DIVERSES
pour fonds, bandes, filets. — Documents.

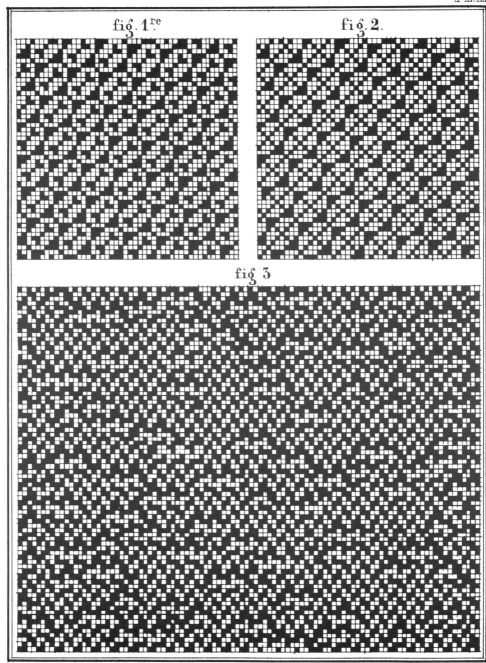

fig. 1re   fig. 2.

fig 3

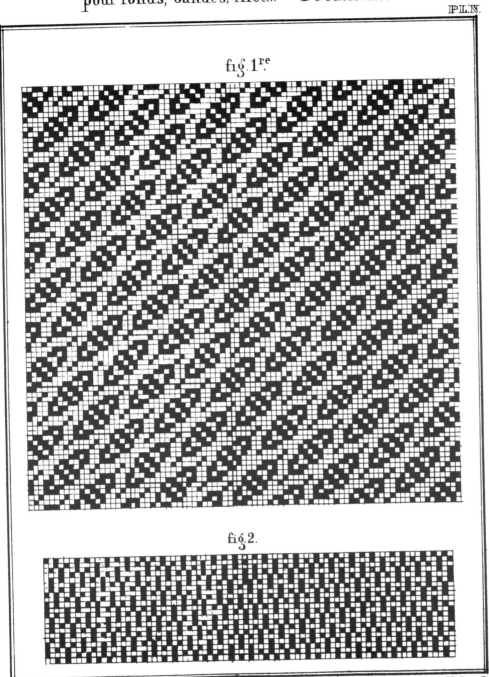

fig.1.re

fig.2.

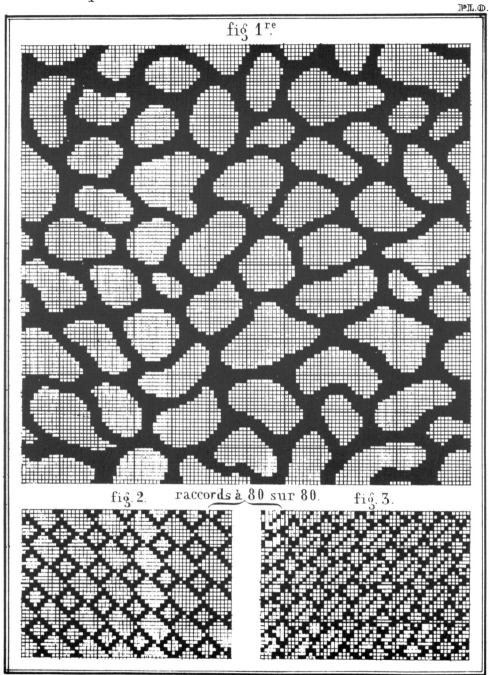

fig 1ʳᵉ

fig. 2.   raccords à 80 sur 80.   fig. 3.

Traité des Tissus. 2ᵉ Edition.   P. FALCOT.   Lith. Boehrer à Altkirch.

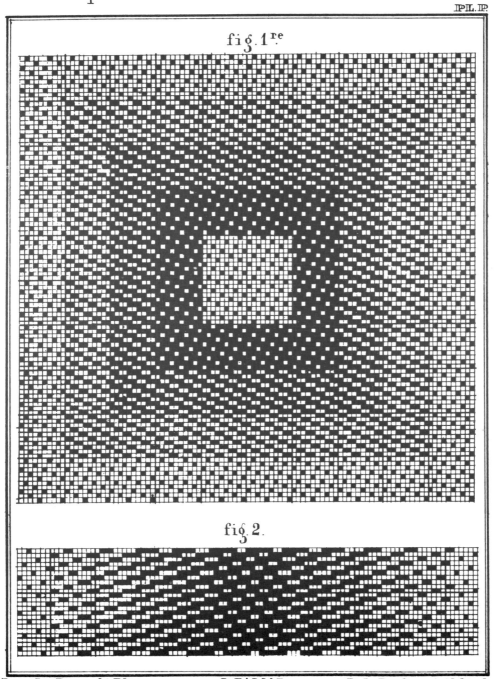

fig.1re

fig.2.

Traité des Tissus. 2.e Edition.   P. FALCOT.   Lith. Boehrer à Altkirch.

ARMURES DIVERSES
pour fonds, bandes, filets. – Documents.

fig. 1 re

fig. 2.

fig. 3.

Traité des Tissus. 2 e Edition.   P. FALCOT.   Lith. Boehrer à Altkirch.

ARMURES DIVERSES
pour fonds, bandes, filets. - Documents.

fig. 1re.
Raccords à 352, sur les deux sens.

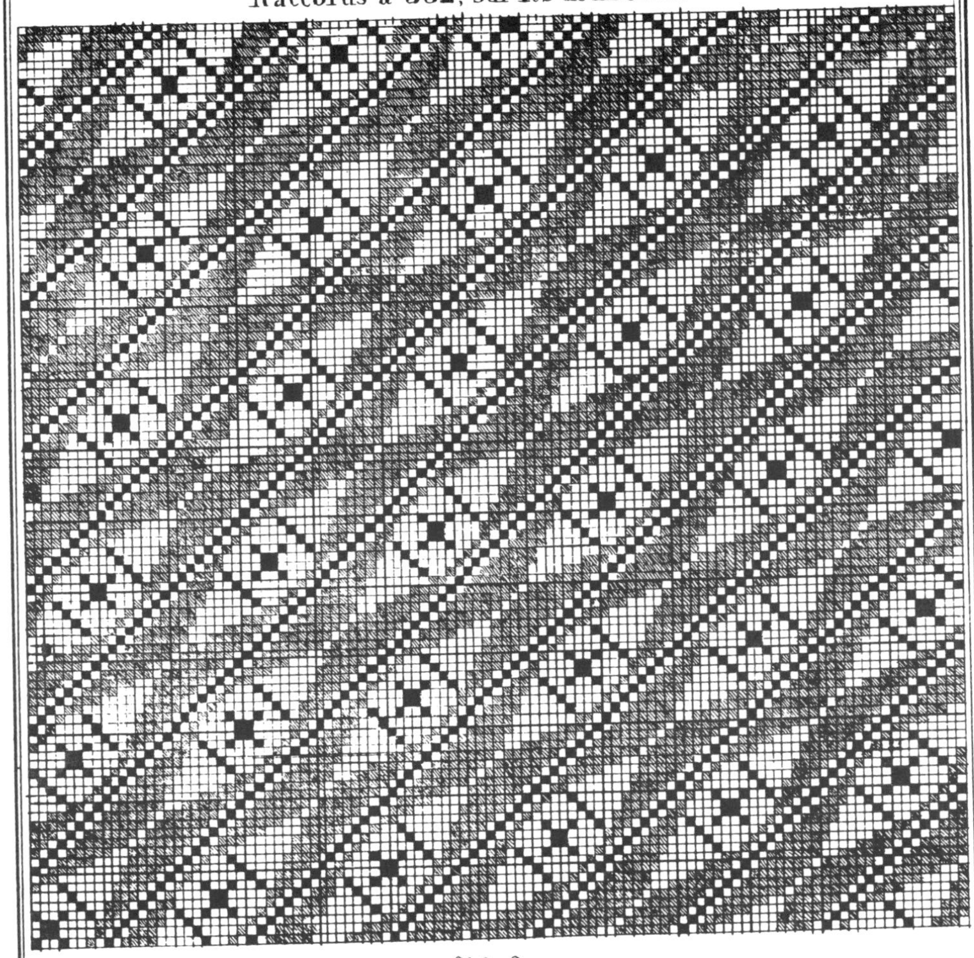

fig. 2.

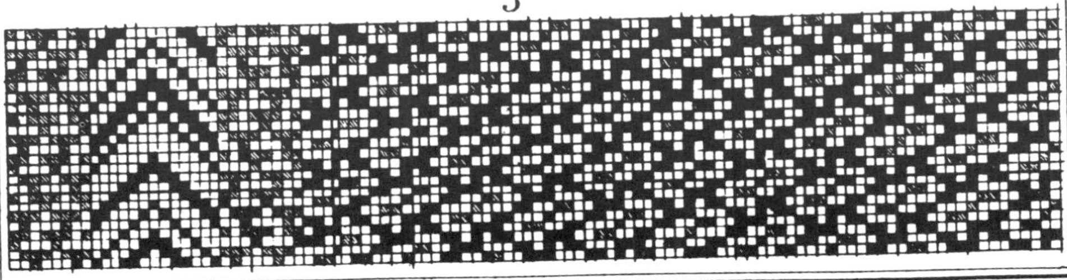

ARMURES DIVERSES
pour fonds, bandes, filets. - Documents.

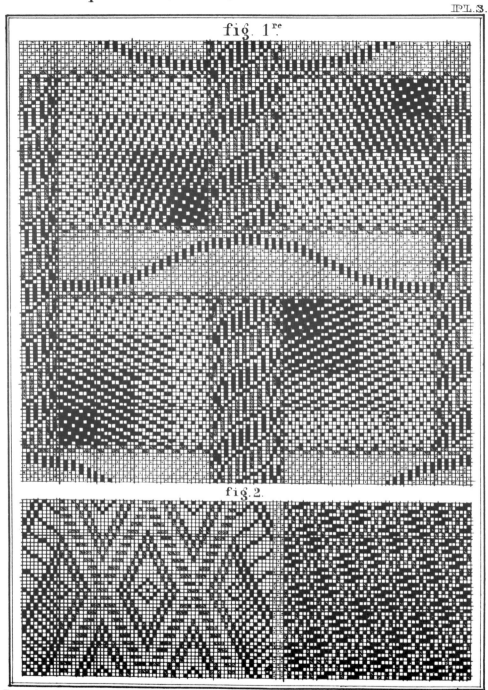

fig. 1ʳᵉ

fig. 2.

Traité des Tissus. 2.ᵉ Edition.   P. FALCOT.   Lith. Boehrer à Altkirch.

ARMURES DIVERSES
pour fonds, bandes, filets. – Documents.

fig. 1.re

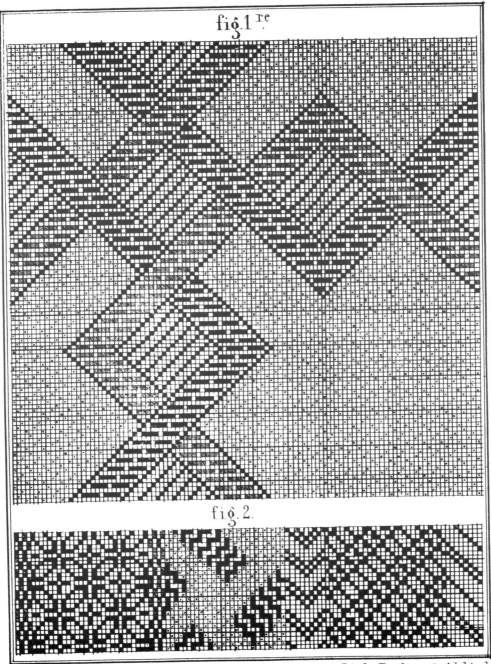

fig. 2.

Traité des Tissus. 2.e Edition.   P. FALCOT.   Lith. Boehrer à Altkirch.

ARMURES DIVERSES
pour fonds, bandes, filets. ~ Documents.

fig. 1.re

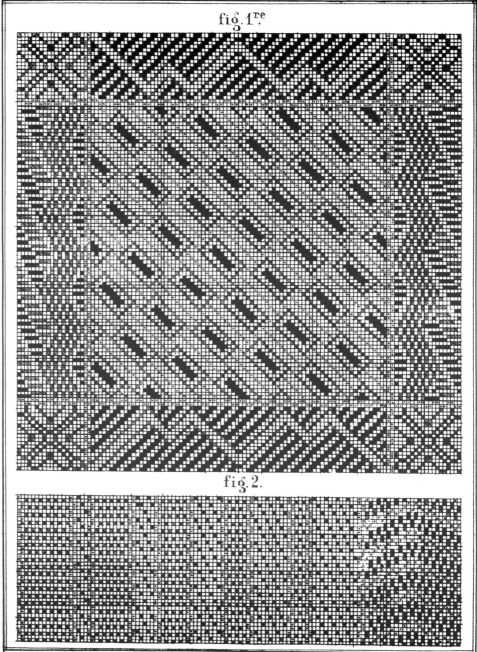

fig. 2.

Traité des Tissus. 2.e Edition.   P. FALCOT.   Lith.Boehrer à Altkirch.

ARMURES DIVERSES
pour fonds, bandes, filets. ~ Documents.

fig 1re

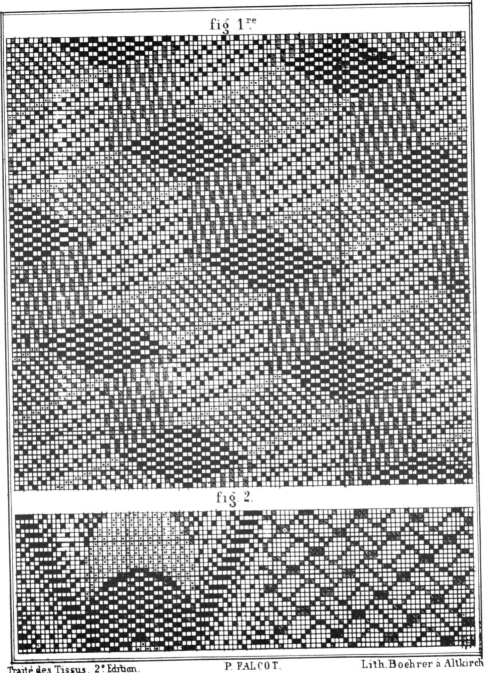

fig. 2.

Traité des Tissus. 2e Edition.   P. FALCOT.   Lith.Boehrer à Altkirch.

ARMURES DIVERSES
pour fonds, bandes, filets. — Documents.

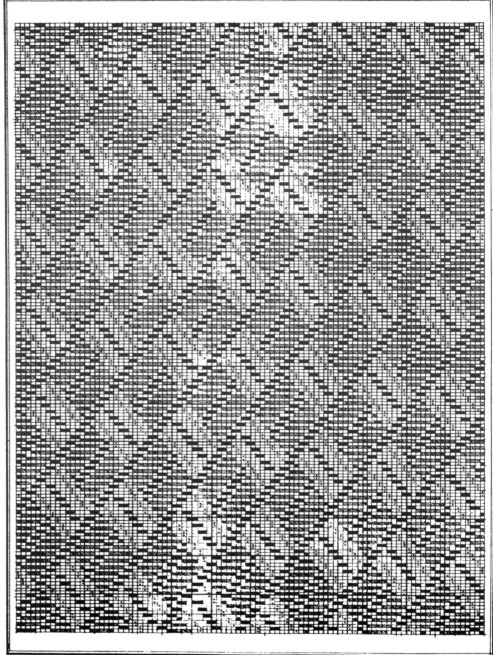

Traité des Tissus. 2ᵉ Edition. **P. FALCOT.** Lith. Boehrer à Altkirch.

ARMURES DIVERSES
pour fonds, bandes, filets. — Documents.

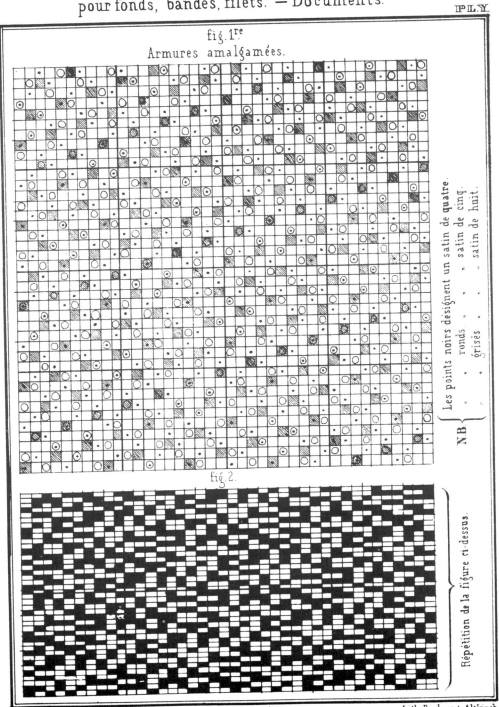

fig. 1re
Armures amalgamées.

fig. 2.

NB { Les points noirs desigñent un satin de quatre.
ronds » satin de cinq.
grisés » » satin de huit.

Répétition de la figure ci-dessus.

ARMURES DIVERSES
pour fonds, bandes, filets. — Documents.

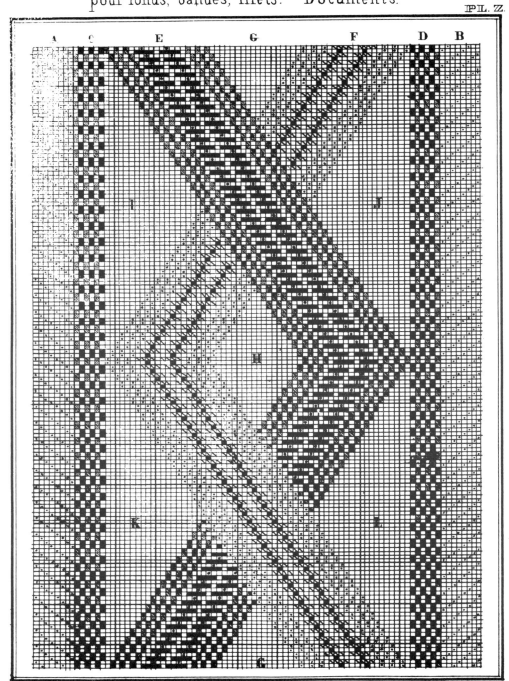